AN
OWNER'S GUIDE

ALL YOU NEED TO KNOW ABOUT YOUR...

STAFFORDSHIRE BULL TERRIER

Clare Lee

Acknowledgements
The publishers would like to thank the following for help with photography:
Steve Halifax, Sharon Pearse and Steve Horsman (Bullhawk), Andy Jones
(Gwynford), Clare Lee (Constones), JoAnn Essex (Javawolf), and Shirley Gray
(Bullmaple).

Cover photo: © Tracy Morgan

The question of gender
The 'he' pronoun is used throughout this book instead of the
rather impersonal 'it', but no gender bias is intended.

ISBN
978-1-906305-49-9
1-906305-49-8

Printed in China through Printworks Int.Ltd.

Contents

The Essential Staffordshire Bull Terrier

The Staffordshire Bull Terrier is a dog of medium size, strongly built, with well developed muscles, a broad head, short coat and a fine, whippy tail. He has a very extrovert character. He cannot be missed powering down the street, usually at the end of his lead. Meeting him in his home he will be effusively friendly. He craves attention and will sit closely beside you to allow easier patting and stroking. Meet him at the park and he may well be chasing hell for leather, to catch a ball or a frisbee. He is a picture of energy, a powerhouse in compact housing.

Wasp, Child and Billy: Detail from a hand-coloured engraving by H.G. Chalon, 1809.

STAFFORD ROOTS

The Stafford is a descendant of the old English Bulldog, who himself was descended from the mastiff type dogs found across Europe, and often referred to, somewhat endearingly, as 'wide mouthed' dogs. Unfortunately for them, these wide mouths were most commonly used for pugnacious and often bloody pastimes for the amusement of their owners. Thus, the Bulldog was most famously used to bait bulls and to a lesser extent bears. We have written and pictorial evidence of these pastimes and the type of dogs used for them. Prints such as Wasp, Child and Billy show us that the Bulldogs of this era bore little resemblance to the modern day Bulldog. They were taller, lighter built animals with strong, broad heads and short muzzles which had some 'lay back' but not to the extremes of the present day dog.

When bull baiting lost its appeal – all these so-called 'sports' seemed to have peaks and troughs of popularity – the focus switched to the 'sport' of dog fighting. For this, a smaller, quicker dog was needed. These were developed either from lighter Bulldogs or by mixing the Bulldog with a terrier of some kind – the most popular candidate being the now extinct

The Westminster Pit.   *Courtesy P. & J. Loughborough.*

English White Terrier. The new dogs became known as Bull and Terriers, but such prints as *The Westminster Pit* show us that the dogs involved in fighting do not differ substantially from the Bulldog type of Crib and Rosa.

The 1835 Cruelty to Animals Act made the UK the first country to make dog fighting illegal. However, under-cover fighting seems to have continued. Indeed, the spy hole in the door on the right of *The Westminster Pit* print suggests that spectators were being scrutinised. The 1911 Protection of Animals Act reinforced the Dog Fighting ban.

At this time, Bull and Terriers were kept in various parts of the UK, especially in mining areas or those where heavy industry flourished. Apart from being used in illegal fighting bouts, they were employed for badger baiting, ratting and such quirky 'sports' as fighting a monkey.

THE LEGACY
The fact that this type of dog survived at all means that it must have had something special to offer to the general public. As they were predominantly owned by the 'lower orders', they would have lived cheek by jowl with their owners, so what was it that made them so attractive? Did the breed survive because of, or

in spite of, its past history?

Firstly, it must be said that most dogs bite from fear. A dog descended from such gladiatorial stock could not afford to be afraid. Secondly, the aggression showed by Bull and Terriers was strictly confined to other dogs. According to the extant Rules and Agreements from the fighting days, at the end of each 'round' the dogs had to be separated by their human handlers and returned to their corners. Looking once again to our Westminster Pit print, we see that these handlers are completely unprotected – indeed, the sleeves of their shirts are rolled up, exposing their bare arms. Obviously they expect that the dogs will immediately differentiate between dog flesh and human contact. There is also evidence that at the end of some fights, especially if the dog lost, he would be handed over to new owners. This made the Stafford a very adaptable type of dog. Finally, to survive in the pit required quite a lot of 'on the spot' thinking if a dog was going to escape a damaging hold from his opponent. Staffords are interesting companions because they have an inherited ability to work things out and think for themselves.

It may surprise the modern reader to realise how much positive emphasis older breeders put upon the past history of the breed. I was brought

Staffords continue to draw big entries at modern dog shows.

up, as most of my generation of Stafford fanatics were, with the understanding that it is because of the breed's history that they are the reliable, human friendly dog that they undoubtedly are. It seems that confusion has arisen in understanding the difference between a dog that is used for fighting another dog, and one that both fights and guards – in other words, where aggression, albeit controlled, may be directed towards humans as well as dogs. The Stafford has never been developed as a guard dog.

Breed Recognition

In the second half of the 19th century, dog shows began to be organised. The Bull Terrier was exhibited at shows as early as 1862. Bull Terrier breeders, especially those interested in the coloured variety, used their Bull and Terrier cousins to a great extent to produce them. After some years the 'Stafford' was deemed to have done his job, and the Bull Terrier fraternity wished to separate the two breeds again. It was as much to do with the Bull Terrier devotees as to the enthusiasm of the Stafford brotherhood that the Staffordshire Bull Terrier was recognised by the Kennel Club as a separate breed in 1935. The first Champions of the breed, Gentleman Jim and Lady Eve, gained their titles at Bath Championship Show in 1939.

In May 1935 a group of fanciers met in the Midlands in Cradley Heath to form a club, to be known as the Staffordshire Bull Terrier Club. It is important to note that there may have been many different types of 'fighting' dog around the UK, but it was the type most prevalent in the Black Country that became the foundation of the breed.

Having formed a club, the fanciers then drew up a Breed Standard. The Standard of any breed is a blueprint of the ideal animal which breeders should aim to produce. There was an immediate problem facing the fanciers who met to draw up this important document. The breed had lain fallow for so long, it was impossible to say that all the animals were 'pure' bred. Bull Terrier blood had already been introduced, but who could tell if other breeds, especially those which may have shown themselves to be good working dogs, had not also been used. Certainly photographs of Bull Terriers and Staffordshire Bull Terriers of the 1930s show a much closer resemblance than examples of the two breeds do today.

The breed fanciers set about collecting records, photographs and sketches of Staffordshire Bull Terriers, and they also called upon what is described as 'the lore and cumulative experience of generations'. They are also recorded as having two dogs, Jim the Dandy and Fearless Joe, present at the meeting.

In spite of the hotch potch that might have gone into producing Staffords over a number of years, they were able to identify features which occurred again and again, even among dogs which might vary in other respects. These features could be termed 'typical' for the breed and were therefore included in the Standard. So, evidently with some unanimity, a Description of the Breed was drawn up and this became the Standard as accepted by the Kennel Club.

The Breed Standard is a picture in words of the 'perfect' Staffordshire Bull Terrier.

THE BREED STANDARD

This 1935 Standard has had one or two alterations over the years but remains the blueprint for the breeders of today. The first amendments came in 1948 and the second in 1987 – on both occasions at the behest of the Kennel Club which, from time to time, has sought uniformity or improvements in the various Breed Standards. All Breed Standards are now the property of the Kennel Club and there is only one Standard for the breed. In overseas countries, if any dispute arises about a Breed Standard it is normal practice to follow the country of origin's Standard for the breed. All the basics of the present-day Standard for the Staffordshire Bull Terrier are as laid down in that first description of the breed.

A Breed Standard was drawn up to describe the 'ideal' Staffordshire Bull Terrier.

General appearance

The Breed Standard starts with a description of the general appearance of the dog – a sort of pen picture. The first thing that strikes you on meeting a Stafford is that he has a very short, shiny coat that ripples with muscle which makes him feel hard to the touch. He should also be 'balanced' – a doggy term which is hard to explain but in general means that all his parts should look as though

A sound and reliable temperament is a hallmark of the breed.

they belong together. If you look at a Stafford – particularly where he stands among others of his own breed – and you think: 'what long legs he has' or conversely: 'how short and stubby he looks' then he is not balanced.

A key to the difference between a good Stafford and an outstanding one is the balance between the two characteristics that the Standard stresses – strength and agility. It is comparatively easy to breed a dog built like a weightlifter, but such a dog may not look active or agile. Conversely, it is even easier to produce a lightweight dog that can skip across the fields and dales, but looks as though a good strong wind would knock him over. Mixing the Bull and the Terrier correctly is a difficult task, but it is a goal that all breeders should aim for.

The easy cop-out is to veer towards one extreme or the other, but the rewards, if you can hit it right, are well worth the effort. The Stafford must show great strength for his comparatively small size, but at the same time he must look like an agile, active animal.

Characteristics and temperament
For me, this is the most important part of the Standard. If you don't have the correct characteristics and

A Stafford's head is what makes him unique in the dog world.

temperament, you have lost the very essence of the Stafford – no matter how physically correct he might be.

As previously stated, the Stafford has inherited certain characteristics from his forebears. First is courage – and we must acknowledge what a positive attribute this is for any dog, especially in this fast and noisy modern age. Aggression can be taught and often stems from insecurity, but courage is 'bred in the bone' and is represented by a sensible, confident dog. The Stafford also has stability and, as previously discussed, he is a very smart dog well capable of thinking for himself. I attended 'character tests' of Staffords in Sweden, and I found out how

outstandingly good the breed is at overcoming and forgetting bad experiences. This is the basis for their cheerful, stable, and fearless temperament.

This is virtually the only Breed Standard that asks that the dog be friendly especially with children. In some countries he is called the 'nanny dog'. There certainly is a bond between a Stafford and a child.

Being bold and fearless is a way of saying a a Stafford should be 'bombproof' and able to face up to all trials and tribulations. However, he was never supposed to be a guard, and is usually useless as one. Because of his love of children and indeed anything that is weaker, his

The Stafford Nose

A good Stafford has a pretty large nose and this must be black. The red or 'Dudley' nose has always been frowned upon, and in the first Standard it debarred a dog from winning any prize. Occasionally a blue puppy will lose the pigment in his nose as he matures and the nose becomes slate grey in colour. Some pied puppies are born with pink or pink/black noses. Over the first few weeks of life, these should become completely black. Failure to do so is termed a 'butterfly' nose and is a fault.

ability to think for himself can mean that he will, of his own accord, protect a child in danger.

Head

If we now start to go over the various parts of the dog, we should start at the beginning – the head. The 1935 Standard had a scale of points and in this no less than 30 of the 100 points was awarded to the head – which shows its importance. The head is a Stafford's most distinctive attribute – it marks him out as a Stafford and no other breed.

The head is broad but must be in balance with the rest of the body – a Stafford should not look like a tadpole. It must have strength, which means it is deep as well as broad, and that depth is particularly important in the foreface. The ratio of the foreface to skull is roughly one-third foreface to two-thirds skull. These measurements are taken from the end of the nose to the stop (the step-up from the muzzle to the skull), and from the stop to the occiput bone at the base of the skull. These measurements are done in straight lines.

Looked at from above, the head tapers slightly to the nose, but this must only be gradual as a very pointed 'snipey' foreface is not desirable. The bone structure on the head is the basis for a lot of muscle development. Over the skull this musculation forms a line or furrow down the middle of the skull. At the side of the head there should be distinct muscles or 'cheek bumps'.

The stop is the pivot of the head. When a Stafford has the correct stop, the plane of his muzzle and that of his skull will almost be parallel. If the stop is too pronounced, the nose is higher than the stop and the dog is called 'dish faced' – the extreme of this is seen in the Boxer or the Bulldog. If the stop is not properly defined then the head is termed 'down faced' – the extreme here being the Bull Terrier or the Borzoi.

The Stafford's head should be 'clean' – that is, there should be no loose flesh, sponginess around the muzzle or wrinkle on the foreface.

Eyes

With so much Bull Terrier blood behind the Stafford, it is not unusual to see an almond shaped eye, but this is not ideal and alters the expression of the animal, to its detriment. In breeds where the stop is extreme, the eye is bulbous (e.g. the Bulldog), but where the stop is shallow or non-existent, the eye is deep-set and triangular (e.g. the Bull Terrier). Where the Stafford has a correctly defined stop his eye will be round and set to look straight ahead, neither deep-set nor bulbous. This gives the Stafford its essential look, which is bold but kind.

An interesting sideline to the eye being placed to look straight ahead is that the Stafford is wonderful at judging distance, and a dab hand at 'catching'. I have great fun throwing treats for my

The eyes are positioned at the front of the head, which makes the Stafford very good at judging distance.

dogs – of course you need to have them sitting or stationed at a fair distance from one another so that they don't try to catch the other's treat!

The eyes should be dark in colour. There is a codicil that the colour may 'bear some relation to coat colour'. This causes concern with novices – for example, should a white dog have a white eye? In fact, this is a sensible warning as a brown eye in a red dog may look perfect, whereas the same dark brown eye colour in a black dog may look a little light. It is important to use some common sense when applying this part of the Standard. The really undesirable eye colours are yellow, blue or green. Eye rims should be dark, although it is permissible for a dog with white colouring around its eye or eyes to have pink eye rims.

Half-prick or 'rose' ears should be set at the side of the head.

Ears

The ears of the Stafford should be set at the side of the head. Where the Bull Terrier influence has been strong, the ears tend to be placed high on the top of the skull with little space between. The best ear carriage is 'rose' although half prick is allowed. Full prick ears were allowable in the 1935 Standard, as because of the Bull Terrier infusion there were many prick eared Staffords in the early days, but they are not permissible in today's Standard.

A rose ear has a crease which runs across the ear from its base, taking it in a backward direction. This then folds forward to the top edge of the ear. In a half-prick ear, the crease is not defined and the tip of the ear just turns over and forward.

Ears should be small and thin. Large heavy ears spoil the expression of the head. Good ears help a good head to look a super head. Unfortunately, the reverse can be said for poor ears – especially where they are large, thick and heavy.

Mouth

The lips in particular should be tight to the jaws and never hang down below the lower jaw. The jaws are big and strong and large enough to house large teeth. The teeth should be arranged in a perfect scissor bite, which means that the upper teeth

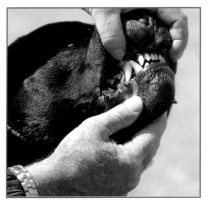

The Stafford has large teeth, meeting in a scissor bite, and a powerful jaw.

closely overlap the lower teeth.

Because of the Bulldog ancestry the undershot mouth – where the bottom teeth or jaw are in front of the top – is quite prevalent in the breed although not as common as in years gone by. This does not harm a dog for normal living but is considered a fault in the show ring. The pronounced 'overshot' mouth, where the top jaw is so far in front of the bottom that a gap is created, is more of a fault since it creates another problem – a narrow, weak underjaw.

In a correct mouth, the large canine teeth on the bottom jaw should fit snugly behind the top incisors. Where they are not clearly visible, they may grow up into the roof of the dog's mouth, resulting in inverted or converging canines. This is a fault and could be most uncomfortable for the dog concerned. Where the dog has a wide, strong foreface, the front teeth will appear to be in a straight-line. The teeth should never slant backwards or forewards from the gums but be set square to the jaw.

Neck
The Stafford is unlike most of the terrier breeds in that its Standard does not ask for a 'reach' of neck. In fact, quite the reverse, since the Standard says that the neck should be 'rather short'. This does not mean that there should be no length of neck but certainly eliminates a long, ewe-like reach of neck as is seen in some other terriers.

Forequarters
Unlike most breeds, the Stafford is shown face-on. This draws attention to his forequarters. The front legs should be straight from the elbow to the pasterns. There is discernable muscle on the front legs and the bone should be substantial – but not flat or coarse.

The front should be wide. This sometimes causes problems for students of fighting breeds who see that many of these are narrow at the front. The point is that the Bull and Terrier in the Black Country was distinguishable for being a shorter, wider dog than many others. His strength apparently being that it was hard to knock him off his feet. The modern-day Stafford has kept this strong base and, in its turn, this base is dependant upon the way his shoulders are formed – to be precise, the angulation between the shoulder blade and the humerus or bone of the upper arm.

People try to impress with angle measuring, but it is usually best to use your eyes before you analyse what they are telling you. In simple terms, if you look at a breed like the Bulldog then his shoulders are so 'layed back' i.e. the angle is so wide that his body is virtually slung between his legs. Conversely looking at a running dog, such as a Lurcher, the shoulders are so 'upright' that the front cannot be anything other than narrow. The Stafford's front should lie between these two extremes. Where the shoulders are correct then the point of the elbows will go straight back – neither pointing inwards nor outwards.

One very typical characteristic of the Stafford, which is sometimes over-looked, is that that the front feet should turn out a little and not point straight ahead or inwards. In order for this to happen, there is a slight backwards slope from the foot to the wrist that allows the feet to turn out slightly. This should not be confused with weak pasterns where the whole foot looks flat. With the correct lay-

The front should be wide, giving the Stafford a strong base.

back and slight turn out the pastern is very springy and resilient – ideal for an active and agile dog.

Body

The body of the Stafford is best assessed from above and from the side. From above, you get a clear picture of his spring of rib; this should not be over-done, but yet he must not be flat or 'slab' sided. From behind the ribs, his waist should be nipped in before the swell of his well-muscled hindquarters. This definition of his body is a very characteristic attribute of a good Stafford.

The Stafford's ribcage is fairly long but his couplings – that is the unprotected part of his belly from the end of his last rib to the start of his hind legs – should be short. It is not desirable to breed for ultra short backs as this produces a less flexible animal – often such dogs have to swing their hind legs in order to move forward.

A level topline is an important element of the ideal Stafford. Some breeds have sway or a dip in their backs – this is not desirable in the Stafford. Alternatively others have a curved or 'roach' back – again, an undesirable trait in a Stafford. A fit Stafford will often have a crest of muscle over his hindquarters but he should never fall away over the hindquarters.

Interestingly, where a Stafford is too heavy, you are more likely to see a dip in his back whereas where he is too lightly built you are most likely to see the roach or Whippet-like topline. This clause of the Standard also mentions width again, so there can be no doubting that throughout the ages

The ribcage is long, and the topline is level.

men have looked for a rather wide front in a good Stafford.

Looking from the side is the way to see the length or shortness of a Stafford. But another thing you can check is the depth of his brisket. The ideal is where the brisket – or lowest edge of the ribs – ends just a tad below the elbow. Where the brisket comes well below the elbow, the dog will appear too heavy and 'cloddy'. Where this point is above the elbow then the dog will appear to be too light and as if he is on stilts. This was not the original dog that was hard to knock off his feet!

The hindquarters are the Stafford's powerhouse.

Hindquarters

Many people comment upon the hindquarters of the Stafford – mainly because in a fit dog these are firmly muscled. In fact, the firmness or even hardness to the touch of a Stafford in fit condition is something that breeders are proud of. The hindquarters are the Stafford's powerhouse. He drives himself forwards on the move and, in play, these are the pistons that allow jumping to amazing heights.

The stifles should be well bent and where this occurs the hock will turn down towards the ground. There is therefore a nice curve to the dog's hind legs. If the stifle is not bent then his legs appear to be in a straight line, and the hocks are forced to point up in the air. It is also quite common to see the reverse, where the hind legs are over-angulated. Here, the hind legs of the dog will stretch out behind him with the hocks well beyond the pelvis. Such a dog is at a disadvantage in the running and jumping stakes as he will have to 'collect his legs' before he can propel himself forward. A correctly-built Stafford is like a coiled spring and can snap into action instantly.

Looking from behind the dog, his legs must be parallel. If his hocks turn in towards each other he is called 'cow hocked', and if the hocks turn out he is called 'pin toed' as the toes are forced inwards towards one another.

Feet

A lot of attention should be paid to a Stafford's feet. At the front they should be halfway between the cat and the hare in size. The small, neat cat foot, well knuckled up is attractive superficially but a larger, clumpier foot is more able to grip the ground in a tussle. The hare foot is usually associated with poor bone and splayed toes. Very often such a foot – with its long toes – does not sufficiently rub against the floor and cause problems for the owners when nails become too long.

With the clumpier foot come thick pads – another desirable feature, giving him stability. The nails should be black, unless there is white on the toes in which case they may be pink. A well constructed foot should rarely if ever need nail cutting once the dog is out of puppyhood.

Movement should be free and purposeful.

Tail

Most of the Stafford Standard is couched in pretty down to earth terms. However, when they got to the tail the fanciers suddenly waxed lyrical with talk such as 'should not curl much and may be likened to an old-fashioned pump handle'. It is a thin, tapering tail, and in the UK, it is common to accentuate this in the show ring by trimming the hairs off the tail.

The ideal length is generally accepted as reaching – when held straight – to the hock or just below, and it is quite thick at the base. The tail must be set low, which means that the tail emerges from the hip bones, covers the anus and slopes down in a gentle curve. It must be said that a tail set too high does spoil the balance of the dog.

Movement

A movement clause was only included in the Staffordshire Bull Terrier Standard in 1987 – quite surprising when you consider that this is an 'active and agile dog' according to part one of the Standard.

The keynote for the correct movement of a Stafford is that it is free and purposeful. At the front he should lift his front legs only slightly off the ground – that is with an economy of movement. It might look pretty if he prances or moves like a hackney horse but it is not typical. We could hear the click, click of the front feet on one of our best moving dogs every time he crossed the kitchen floor.

The rear is where the real action takes place, and this is why he needs his muscles. The rear legs go straight into the tracks of the front. Providing that he is well constructed, you will virtually see a tunnel between his front and rear legs when he walks away from or towards you. If he is cow hocked or pin toed then his rear legs will mask his front. If his shoulder placement is wrong then he may well approach you with forelegs crossing or elbows pointing outwards. Good handlers in the show ring can hide many faults or failings in their charges when standing, but once on the move the dog is on his own!

It is in the movement phase that the Stafford is seen to be very different from the average terrier. He moves with such forcefulness and power from the rear. He drives himself forwards rather than daintily springing up and down along the ground. The Stafford also has a happy knack of moving at two different speeds – and if you don't get the proper speed for him he may well start to roll rather than drive along. So, if you intend to show your dog, do practice the speed at which you walk him until you are sure that you are

getting the right speed for him to really show his paces!

Coat

The Stafford's coat is short; the hairs lie close to his skin and if he is in good condition it will shine like satin. It should fit closely and not have any wrinkles or folds so that it shows off all his muscle and accentuates the definition of his body.

Colour

We are so lucky in Staffords that we have such a variety of colours. The basic colours are tan and black with their dilute forms fawn and blue. Brindle is a pattern and so we have a

Mahogany Brindle.

wide variety of very pretty brindle colours from silver to mahogany, depending on the arrangement of the tan to the black hairs.

Blue was not mentioned as a colour for Staffords in the 1935 Standard. They are now very common as pets, but not so often seen in the ring as the colouration is often accompanied by an undesirable feature, such as a slate-grey nose or yellow eye.

All-white Staffords, as all-black Staffords, are rarely seen but they do crop up now and again. Red or brindle pied – that is predominantly white

Red and white.

dogs with some brindle or red (tan) patches – are popular. The tan colourings vary from deep red to the dilute pale fawn.

Liver – a very deep red colour – which is often accompanied by green eyes and brown noses, is considered a fault as is the black-and-tan colour in a Stafford. Red Staffords with white chests and black masks are permissible. But a Stafford should not be tri-coloured i.e. red, black and white colouring throughout.

Height and Weight

There has been much written about the height and weight of the Stafford, chiefly because in the revised 1948 Standard the height was lowered from a range of 16-18 inches (40.5-45.7 cm) down to 14-16 inches (35.5-40.5 cm). In fact, this did not mean that half the Stafford population were debarred from the show ring as most were around the 16 inch (40.5 cm) mark anyway. One of the shortest Stafford Champions of all times, Ch. Head Lad of Vilmar, advertised at 14 inches (36.8 cm) and did his winning long before the change in the Standard. The change came to keep the Standard in tune with the dog as it existed. As time has progressed many of us have reason to bless the reduction. Anyone wanting a guard dog will look for an animal taller than 16 inches, and that suits us fine as

Skewbald.

the Stafford is not a natural guard anyway. All these measurements are taken from the ground to the withers i.e the highest point of the shoulders.

As for the weight, the Standard states: dogs 13-17kg (28-38lb); bitches 11-15.4 kg (24-34 lb). People often question the accuracy of the weight for the 1935 Standard – were these fighting weights? In any case, the advent of modern feeding methods has altered everything. Looking back to my childhood, no one had access to the puppy milk, foods and additives that we frequently give our in-whelp bitches and puppies now. Then, if the pups managed to get through to four weeks, they would be full of worms and subject to the most arduous worming process whereby the medicines completely scoured the little things. If they survived that, they came out the other end a good pound lighter to face home-baked rusks and scraps from the table. I would love to be able to bring some of those old dogs back, feed them a modern diet and see what weight they end up at.

Note

All Kennel Club Standards require that male dogs are 'entire' – that is, that they have two apparently normal and fully descended testicles, whatever the breed.

Summing up

The Staffordshire Bull Terrier has survived many vicissitudes since it was recognised in 1935. Throughout, the breed has maintained its own particular character and its physical appearance has altered very little. The Stafford is still an easy maintenance, healthy, natural, no-nonsense sort of dog. Long may it continue to give us pleasure and affection.

Choosing a Stafford

When my husband and I kept a boarding kennel, we were amazed at the number of people who had quite simply chosen the wrong type of dog for their lifestyle. The lady who hated grooming yet had chosen a Tibetan Terrier, the couple who disliked walking but had bought a Pointer, the flat dweller who selected a Border Collie – bred on a farm to boot. Rescue kennels are full of the fall-out from such mistakes.

It is a very good idea to study the various breeds before making a final choice. The Stafford is a very versatile breed – in some countries it is called 'the nanny dog' and in others the 'all purpose dog'. Those of us who love them wouldn't keep any other kind of dog, but even we have to admit that it is not the ideal companion for everyone or every circumstance.

TTHE PROS AND CONS

The Staffordshire Bull Terrier is a medium-sized dog, with a short easy-to-care-for coat. He is physically very strong and, as a breed, they suffer from few hereditary problems. Our vet says he would go bankrupt if he saw all his clients as infrequently as he saw our dogs. The Stafford's character makes him extremely human friendly and he has a special affinity for children. He is intelligent and fun. These are some of the many 'pros' in favour of you choosing a Stafford.

But there are 'cons'. Whilst he is not very tall he is very strong; most people find that just looking at a Stafford gives them little idea of his strength. You really need to take a Stafford for a walk or generally handle him to fully appreciate his physical strength. Although he may love children, it is not advisable to let a young child exercise a Stafford unsupervised because of his strength.

Although a Stafford has a very strong constitution, he is prone to accidents because he tends to be headstrong. Broken legs, strained joints and road accidents are the main causes of a Stafford going to a vet. We always advise an owner to take out pet insurance when buying a new puppy.

Because of their confident, jolly outlook on life, a Stafford will show his love for the human race in a very exuberant manner. He will always fuss visitors, yearning to be stroked

If you are looking for a guard dog, choose another breed.

Male or female?

If you are sure you have enough energy, forbearance and sense of humour to take on a Stafford, then your next choice must be of which sex. The male of any breed, with his high testosterone level, is more inclined to be dominant, especially in any tussle with another dog. On the other hand, if trained properly, a male makes the more interesting, and often the more loyal, companion.

Stafford bitches can also fall out with other dogs, although not so violently or frequently. They are usually more 'self centred' than males. Perhaps because they would be the ones to raise the next generation, they tend to have a better idea of what is 'best' for them.

and petted. He can never be termed 'aloof' or 'reserved' as are some other breeds. Unfortunately, as a result they are easy victims of dog nappers.

A Stafford is not always friendly to other animals. This can be minimised by socialisation early in life, but there will always be that possibility that if he is challenged he may respond. You must be prepared for this and ready to be on your guard.

Like most dogs, a young Stafford will chew things – especially at teething time. Because of his strong jaws a Stafford can do a lot more damage than most other breeds. Stories of them demolishing door jambs, even chewing through doors, is not uncommon. I know of one owner who, having had the leg of his antique dining table almost chewed through, resorted to chopping off the undamaged three legs. Not all of us can be so tolerant.

I was recently contacted by a new

A female Stafford will play with a ball just as long as it interests her, and will then walk away to find a better amusement. They are often more greedy than the males.

Bitches will have twice-yearly 'season' or 'heats' which can cause problems if there are many dogs in your area and especially if these are allowed to roam. Most vets will spay bitches before their first season – there are some medical advantages for this such as a reduced risk of mammary tumours. It is not necessary for a bitch to have a litter. This will not 'fulfil' her – that is giving dogs human feelings. Nor would I advise using a dog at stud unless you are able to offer him a steady supply of bitches, which will involve showing him successfully. In general, dogs not used at stud will settle down after 'puberty' and will not hanker after what they have not known. Conversely, once used at stud he will be more likely to look for, and run after, another bitch.

owner who said he was having trouble with training his young Stafford. "All I want is a calm, submissive dog," he said. I could only tell him that he had chosen the wrong breed. If you want a dog who will sit quietly in his bed and ignore your visitors then this is not the dog for you.

Another common misconception among people buying a Stafford is the belief that they will prove to be good guards. They were never developed as guards and many finish in rescue because they have disappointed their owners in this respect. Some will, for some unknown reason, guard a car by barking if anyone approaches the windows. They also have a natural instinct to protect a child or any weaker member of the family. We know of a friend's child who, when he feared chastisement for some misdeed, would take himself off to the dog's bed and seek protection from the dog – much to his father's frustration.

If you want to keep two Staffords it is best to avoid two males.

MORE THAN ONE?

It is not a good idea to buy two puppies from the same litter or indeed to have two Staffords who are close in age. Training, socialising and general bonding is much harder to achieve. The one-to-one relationship between a Stafford and his owner is the ideal.

If you already have another dog in the family, then it may be best to select the opposite sex for your new puppy. In general it will be easy to introduce a bitch puppy to another bitch or to an adult dog. But it is definitely not a good idea to try to run two male animals together – unless there is a great difference in age. The male dominance issue will raise its head one day and many Staffords end up in rescue as a result of their owners being encouraged to have two male Staffords in the one family.

Socialising with other dogs outside the family at an early age is essential. But always make sure that the dogs he meets are friendly.

Other Pets

Staffords will live with cats, rabbits and other small animals if introduced when they are young and if the introductions are carefully supervised. However, it is important to bear in mind that even though your Stafford likes your own cat, he may well take exception to the neighbour's cat if it strays into your garden.

A Stafford can remember if he is beaten up when young and will be on his toes to get his revenge when he is older – a revenge on all dogs, or maybe just the ones that remind him of his original aggressor.

AN OLDER DOG

Having a puppy in the house is hard work, and some people prefer to take on an older, fully trained dog. There are advantages in getting a mature dog, apart from the hope that he is house trained and finished with chewing. The character of the dog is now obvious. So if you love walking and the outdoor life, a very lively, active Stafford could be for you. On the other hand if you are more housebound, a quiet older Stafford could be just the thing.

There are a number of excellent breed rescue groups as well as the more well-known national animal rescue organisations to help you. The Kennel Club issues a booklet with details of every breed's rescue organisations. These groups have to be recommended by a breed club, before they are accepted on to the Kennel Club register of rescue groups.

Workers from the rescue group will want to check your home conditions and your attitude to the breed. In turn, they should be able to give you some idea of the history of the dog on offer or alternatively have a fair idea of his character if he has been assessed in one of their kennels. You will be required to neuter your new charge.

Any dog needs a great deal of time and a lot of committment. The lessons he learns in the first few months of his life will affect him for the rest of his mature years. At times you may begin to think that he will 'never learn this lesson' but perseverance on your part will pay off when you find you own a well adjusted, happy dog that is a

You may prefer to cut out the puppy stage and take on an older dog.

pleasure to live with. Of course, if you take an older dog who has some problems then you have to put extra time into his re-training. Often the rescue group will be able to give you expert advice.

EXERCISE REQUIREMENTS

Staffords do not need miles and miles of exercise – although if you have the time and the inclination they will definitely appreciate it. A dog like a Border Collie, especially one from farm stock, really must have miles of free running. A Stafford can be very happy with a short walk and a quarter of an hour chasing a ball – violent exercise is what suits him best. A Stafford will also take to road walking which helps to keep his nails short, and while he is young gives him experience of the outside world.

FINDING A STAFFORD

Having decided that you really would like a Stafford and that you have a Stafford friendly home, the next most important question is where to source it from. Never has that consideration been more important than it is today.

There are many different 'types' of Staffordshire Bull Terriers advertised in many outlets from the internet to the free papers. It must therefore be stressed that there is only one recognised breed of Staffordshire Bull Terrier, and the best way for you to track down a litter is to contact your local Staffordshire Bull Terrier Breed Club. The Secretary for each of these – and there are 18 throughout Great Britain and Northern Ireland – can be obtained by writing to the Kennel Club in London, by looking on their website, or in one of the national dog papers.

The term 'breeder' covers such a wide spectrum – from the pet owner who decides to have one litter from their bitch up to the person who has been breeding for the show ring for many years and over many generations. In between are those who have a little knowledge but not a great deal of experience, and those who have a lot of experience in producing numerous litters, but who are only interested in breeding as an extra form of income.

If you contact the secretary of a breed club, it should maximise your chances of finding a 'proper' and caring breeder. Even so, I advise you to approach the selection of your puppy with you head and not your heart.

A good, reputable breeder will want to find out as much as he can about you. If the only thought is: 'have you got the money?' then that

The Stafford enjoys short, violent bursts of exercise.

breeder is best left alone. A puppy that is registered with the Kennel Club should come not only with a pedigree – this on its own is only a number of names on a piece of paper – but also with a registration document. Make sure that the documents are issued by the Kennel Club in London. People have been known to start their own kennel club and registration system from their own front rooms.

Viewing the Puppies

When you visit the puppies they should be well housed. This means ideally for a Stafford that they are in the house which will give them the maximum amount of socialisation and ensure that they are well used to the noises of the house – washing machines, vacuum cleaners etc. If they are housed outside, try to assure yourself that they have had plenty of visits from the family and look as though they are used to being handled and played with.

Whether in the house or outside, the living quarters should be as clean as possible. Puppies make a mess, but there should be adequate facilities for disinfecting their quarters. Puppies who are allowed or left to wallow in their own dirt often grow into dirty adults.

The puppies should look healthy. They should have shiny coats, be full of life and not have swollen tummies. Extended tummies are a sign of worms. A good breeder will give you a diet sheet plus a note as to when and how the puppies were wormed.

Make sure that you see the mother and that she is of a sound and happy temperament. A Stafford mother may well be very defensive of her puppies while their eyes are closed – that is before 10 days old. As a result, a caring breeder will not want you to visit at this time. Once the puppies have opened their eyes and are beginning to explore, the mother should be happy for you to

It is important to see the mother with her puppies.

Watch the puppies play together so you can get some idea of their individual personalities.

look at her puppies.

The father may not be present on the premises. Most breeders will need to travel in order to find the right mate for their bitch. Only occasionally will a breeder be lucky enough to own a dog that absolutely suits their bitch. I would be wary if I found that a breeder had a number of bitches, all mated to his own dog, and that dog had little or no recognition in the show ring. My suspicion would be that this is a breeder who is churning out puppies for the money.

You should expect the puppies to come straight out to greet you, wagging their tails. Please do not go to see a litter in your best skirt, stockings and high heels. Many breeders will put that as a black mark against you, since it shows ignorance of the liveliness of young puppies.

Do not be tempted to fall in love with the one who hides in the corner. Properly reared Stafford puppies are confident and out-going. Also be wary of one that is considerably smaller than its litter mates. It may be just a late starter, but it may also have some underlying problem. Time will tell which of these scenarios is correct, but it should be the responsibility of the breeder to keep this type of puppy long enough to see how he turns out.

Health issues affecting Staffords

On the registration papers given to you, the Kennel Club will have included tests for hereditary diseases the parents have had. The Stafford has three main problems. A brain condition L2Hydroxyglutaric aciduria (L-2-HGA) for which there is a DNA test. There are also two eye problems – Hereditary Juvenile Cataracts (HC) for which there is also a DNA test, and Persistent Hyperplastic Primary Vitreous (PHPV) for which, unfortunately there is no DNA test at present. However, there is a test for its presence in a dog, and this examination can be performed on a puppy from six weeks of age.

Hopefully as a result of these tests, your pup will be hereditarily clear. But if the pup comes from a mating where one of the parents is a carrier, you should ask that the pup is tested to decide if it is fully clear, or is itself a carrier. A carrier animal leads a perfectly normal life, but should only be mated to a non-carrier partner. If two carriers are mated together then a percentage of their pups will be affected with the condition – this is why it is essential to check that the parents of any pup you are considering buying have had their DNA tests.

For further information on Stafford health, see Chapter Six: Health Care For Staffords.

It takes an expert eye to pick out a puppy with show potential.

Show Puppy

If you are selecting a puppy with the hope of exhibiting him at shows, you will need to be even more careful with your research. Read as much as you can on the breed, and include at least one book which has a detailed analysis of the Breed Standard. But no matter how well you have prepared yourself, it is advisable to view puppies with a friend who has some knowledge of the finer points of the breed.

Look for a puppy with good bone, squarely built, with a rather wide front and a body that feels quite chunky when you pick him up. Most important of all, make sure that the puppy has a promising head – that is that he has round eyes, set wide apart, and his ears are set on the side and not at the top of his head. His foreface at this stage should be quite blunt – a pointed nose at this age will just get more and more pointed as puppy grows. A head never gets any better than it is at eight weeks old – too often, the head gets weaker.

Do not be carried away by too much salesmanship – especially if it includes promises of a glowing show career. Many Staffords are born every year, but only a very few reach Champion status.

Settling in

S pending a little time thinking about how you want to integrate your new dog into the family will pay dividends in the long run. It is easier to teach new tricks to a dog than to break bad habits and then try to teach new rules. It is a good idea to have a family conference and lay down the house rules before you even collect your puppy.

HOUSE RULES

The first thing that should be decided is where the pup should sleep. Although the Stafford is a strong, 'tough' breed he is particularly susceptible to the cold. Muscle and bone he may have, but he is very short on the protective coat front. Unlike many dogs, a Stafford has no length or density of coat and, unlike many terrier breeds, he does not have a 'double' coat. It follows that you should find a warm and draught free spot for your Stafford's bed.

You must also decide if you want your Stafford to share your furniture. It is tempting to put a little pup beside you on the settee, but will he be as welcome when he is fully grown? Some people give the dog his 'own'

chair, or they are happy to let him share with them, perhaps an extra throw will come in handy to protect the upholstery? Whatever you decide, start as you mean to go on – changing this rule can cause confusion in the dog's mind. From the start make sure that he knows that even if it is 'his' chair, he must come off it if you ask him to.

There may be parts of the house you wish to keep dog free. It must be said that the more freedom a Stafford can enjoy around the house, the more relaxed and well adjusted he will become. But this is not to say that you should not have boundaries. If you don't want him to go upstairs for example, buy a baby gate to prevent access to 'no go' areas.

Staffords are great explorers, so check that the house and garden are safe and secure.

In the garden

Moving to outside the house, the greatest concern here is safety. Ponds, streams and rivers hold a fatal attraction for dogs; Stafford puppies will not be afraid to let their curiosity get the better of them and take a dip.

I would not attempt to keep a Stafford in anything other than an enclosed garden. Even then, the enclosure must be secure. Take a slow tour round the perimeter of your garden and check the fencing or the hedge if that marks the boundary. A Stafford can squeeze through the smallest gap and through the thickest hedges – he is not even put off by thorns, although he may be very dejected afterwards if he is pierced! Make sure that you cover any holes. If you have a fence, it must be high and robust. I had a friend whose Stafford was unable to scale his tall fence, so he simply bulldozered his way through!

You will need a secure gate, preferably bolted from the inside. The danger is not only that your Stafford might wander out and get run over, but unfortunately Staffords are a number one target for dog thieves. They make themselves easy targets because they are so friendly and trusting, even of strangers. So make sure you protect him, as well as protecting your neighbours' gardens from his attentions. Staffords can be enthusiastic diggers, so restrict him to specific areas if you are a dedicated gardener.

A Stafford puppy will soon learn to settle in a crate.

Buying Equipment

Before your pup arrives, you will need to decide what equipment to buy:

Dog Bed

A young Stafford is best suited to having a plastic bed lined with synthetic fleece type blankets. Pretty duvets and soft foam beds may be alright for the older dog, but are far too vulnerable for the teeth of a young, growing Stafford.

Some people like to train their pup from the first to sleep in a cage or crate – even if this is with the door open. A Stafford that is used to such a set up can be easily taken to stay in a stranger's house or in hotels, and will be content to stay in his crate if a visitor comes to the house who is afraid or allergic to dogs. The spaces between the wires of the cage or crate must be smaller than the width of the puppy's jaws, as there is a danger when he is very young of his teeth becoming stuck. A crate for an adult Stafford should be at least 2ft x 2ft x 3ft 6in (60cm x 60cm x 105cm).

Bowls

As well as his bed, your Stafford will need a feeding bowl and a water bowl. Never use your own china for a dog. Stainless steel bowls are the safest to buy – other types may look pretty but they are easily chewed or broken. A pup or an older dog could take it into his head to have a game with his bowl and throw it around, which could prove dangerous if the bowl is breakable.

Food

The breeder will provide you with a diet sheet, and if you can ask for it in advance of getting your puppy you will be able to buy the necessary supplies in readiness (see page 53).

Grooming gear

All Stafford coats benefit from an occasional stiff brush, followed by a rub down with a soft, possibly velvet cloth or grooming glove. A good pair of nail clippers may prove useful and certainly a tooth brush and paste will help keep your pet's teeth in good order.

Some Staffords, especially black brindles, tend to grow thick coats which are longer than normal. To refine this type of coat, hard work with a stripping blade or very harsh brush is necessary.

Collar and Lead

A narrow collar and a lightweight lead are suitable for a young puppy. You can let the puppy wear his collar around the house before taking him out for walks, but do this under supervision as he will try to scratch and get the collar off if he can. When fitting the collar, you should be able to get your fingers between the collar and the neck. If it is any tighter it will cause discomfort; if it is any looser the puppy could pull backwards out of the collar and run away. As a puppy grows and his neck thickens, you will need to buy larger-size collars.

When choosing a lead for a Stafford it is always best to opt for leather rather than chain. It may be a nuisance if your Stafford starts to chew his lead – but train him, with firmness and kindness, not to do this. The half leather/half chain leads are terribly hard on your hands and prevent you using the lead properly. I also find that the flexible type of lead is very useful. These are retractable, nylon leads operated by a button and housed in a plastic carrier which fits into your hand. This allows the dog a fair amount of freedom to sniff and explore, while giving you overall control since you can retract the lead to a short length when necessary. Make sure that any stretch type of lead you choose is of the wider nylon type and is not too fine.

Some dogs react better in a harness – especially if they are bad pullers on the lead – but choose a plain nylon harness and not the the decorated 'fighting' dog type. Harnesses which are decorated with metal badges or shields are emblematic of the fighting dog and therefore give out the wrong message to the general public.

A Stafford can be very destructive so he needs robust toys to play with.

Toys

Most people like to buy toys for their dogs. Balls, frisbees and anything that can be thrown and chased after are very popular with Staffords. He might think that a stick is the best thing of all, but these can be highly dangerous and every year vets see dogs badly injured when, for example, the sharp end of a stick pierces the roof of a dog's mouth.

The key thing with toys for a Stafford is safety. A Stafford can so easily destroy plastic or rubber toys, and small chewed off pieces, or squeaks, can cause lots of problems. The best choice is a really strong, hard rubber ball or a kong. Staffords also like tug toys, but again you must make sure that the tug toy is made of robust material. If you intend to show your pup, it is best to leave pulling toys until he is older as it takes many months for the teeth to be fully set in a dog's gums.

It is not necessary to spend a great deal of money on fancy toys. A dog is often happier playing with the package the expensive toy came in, than reacting to the toy itself. So you can make toys yourself e.g. from old socks. Beware of using tights as these can cause damage internally if swallowed – and they often are. It is also confusing for a dog to be given an 'old' slipper or shoe to chew – very tempting for you to let this happen I know, but how is he going to tell the difference between your 'old' shoe and your smart 'new' pair when they are all the same to him?

ARRIVING HOME

When you go to fetch your pup, take a blanket and some newspaper with you. He may well be sick on the journey home as it will, most probably, be the first time that he has been in a motor vehicle.

On arriving home, let him explore at his own pace – everything is strange and new to him and it will take him a little time to get his bearings. Take him outside and stay with him. Speak to him all the time to encourage him and to make the sound of your voice familiar to him.

MEETING THE FAMILY

If you have children, try to keep them as calm as possible – not an easy task when faced with such an exciting thing as a new puppy. But you can explain to the children the importance of not letting the pup get over excited, plus the dangers of hurting the puppy if they rush around too much. Most dangerous of all is allowing a child to pick up the puppy. Stafford puppies are strong and can easily wriggle free, most especially if the pup is being held by a small child. A fall from any height can cause considerable damage – even broken limbs. So make sure the child is sitting on the floor before being allowed to hold the pup.

Most breeders will not let puppies go at Christmas time to homes where there are children. The excitement and activity in the house is just too great. If a pup gets excited and tries to nip a child – rather as he would his littermates – do not be afraid to tap his nose and say "No". It is important to stop this behaviour before it becomes a problem.

A puppy has a lot to take in when he first arrives in his new home.

Having a pet in a family is a two way process – the dog adds to the fun of family life, but at the same time a child must learn they have a responsibility towards the dog. Even a dog as steady as a Stafford needs a break from play sometimes and puppies, especially, need plenty of time for sleep. Children should therefore be taught right from the outset that when the pup or dog is in his bed, he should be left alone.

The Animal Family

If you already have a pet or pets in your home, you will need to plan how you are going to introduce the newcomer. If you have another dog, it is probably best to make the introduction in the garden. This will be viewed as neutral ground where the puppy cannot immediately take over the resident dog's territory. If the adult dog has toys it particularly loves, it would be best to put them away until

you are sure that the two are on good terms.

Speak to the older animal and reassure him that the pup is something to be accepted by all the family.

Having a Stafford in the family is fun – but children must also be aware of the responsibilities involved.

Finding a vet

It is best to make contact with a vet – find one from personal recommendation if you can – even before you have brought your puppy home. Find out about the regime he follows for inoculations, and when you make your first visit with the puppy you can ask his advice about setting up a worming regime.

It might be that the veterinary practice runs puppy socialising classes so you can sign up for these when your puppy goes for his inoculations. You could also seek your vet's advice about micro-chipping your puppy. If he should stray at any time, having permanent identification will ensure his swift return to you. Permanent and easy identification also helps to protect your Stafford from being stolen.

The resident animal may feel that he is being set aside for the newcomer so remember to give him plenty of pats and lots of talk, even though the endearing youngster is striving to attract all the attention. Be particularly careful at feeding time and when giving any titbits. All interactions with food should be fully supervised.

If you have a cat then, to a large extent, the manner of introduction will be out of your hands. The cat will take the upper-hand in making such decisions as: 'shall we touch noses?' 'shall I allow the puppy to sniff me?' or even, 'shall I stay in the same room as him?' Make sure the cat has places where he can get out of the puppy's way, preferably a higher surface he can escape to. Don't let the puppy tease the cat or he may get a nasty scratch – a simple box round the ears to warn pup off is a necessary lesson. But if pushed too far, the cat might really scratch and if he hits pup's eyes then a really serious injury could result.

It has to be said that while some cats and dogs cuddle up in front of the fire together, many others just learn to tolerate one another – virtually dividing the house up between them. They may have boundaries that the humans in the house just don't realise exist. Whatever the set-up, rest assured that with patience and sensitivity Staffords can live in harmony with most cats.

Small animals such as rabbits, hamsters and birds could be more problematic. It is, after all, natural for a dog to chase a rabbit for food! The best plan is to allow the pup to see the rabbit, hamster or bird while it is in the safety of its hutch or cage, and just observe his reactions. Take things step by step – let the puppy look, sniff, and explore over a number of days so that they are really familiar with each other. In time, the novelty will wear off and most Staffords will lose interest. However, it is better to be safe than sorry, so make sure your Stafford is never left unsupervised in the vicinity of small, caged animals.

FEEDING
You should have received a diet sheet from the breeder. It is really important that you stick to this as far as you possibly can at least for the first few days. A sudden change in diet could upset his tummy which

To begin with, your puppy will need four meals a day.

The first night

The first night that pup is at home can be quite traumatic. Litters of puppies always snuggle up together – often in a great ball with everyone fighting to get on the lowest level and thus be covered by warm littermates. For the first night or even first few nights, the pup will definitely miss his siblings. It is therefore very important that he has a warm, cosy bed. You can also put a hot-water bottle (preferably, if you can get one, a stone type) wrapped tightly in a blanket and not too hot, and place it in the bed. Some people put a ticking clock wrapped in a towel beside pup – the idea being that the tick of the clock will sound like the beat of its littermates' hearts.

The one 'cure' that you should never try – although it has a 100 per cent success rate – is to take pup to bed with you. No breed appreciates a warm bed more than a Stafford. For the sake of avoiding a couple of disturbed nights, you could have a life time of bed sharing. An eight-week-old pup is easily accommodated, but a fully grown Stafford is not.

will make settling in even more stressful for him..

An eight-week-old puppy should be on four meals a day. Two of these – morning and evening – will most probably be of cereal with some form of milk, and the other two meals will be protein of some kind. If pup had been having specially formalised dog milk, then you can gradually change this to cow's milk to make things easier for

Take your puppy out into the garden at regular intervals and he will soon understand what is required.

yourself. A thoughtful breeder may well have started this change over before you collect pup.

As pup grows older he will no longer want four meals; he will tell you this by refusing or not finishing one of his meals. We like to drop the night meal first as this gives a better chance of the puppy being clean through the night.

If you want to change the times or order of the meals do this gradually – it will only take the puppy a couple of days to fit in with the new regime. Puppies are very quick learners.

HOUSE TRAINING

The most important lesson your puppy now has to learn is house training. Nothing is worse than a dirty dog. Staffords in general are clean animals, and having kept a couple of breeds other than Staffords I have learnt to appreciate their natural cleanliness. Right from an early age, a Stafford pup will not want to soil the bed on which he sleeps. He will drag himself off his blanket to the bit of paper that is beyond.

So your Stafford puppy should learn quite quickly to perform outside. Take him out as soon as he wakes from a sleep. Stay with him and when he performs praise him enthusiastically. Do the same routine after he has eaten, or after a play session. Try to use a special word, such as "Busy". In time he will actually begin to perform on command and this is most useful when you are travelling and have only a few comfort stops – usually, of course, determined by the human family!

Staffords notoriously dislike the rain and will try to hang on or sit shivering on the doorstep rather than venture outside in the wet. However, I am afraid you have to harden your heart, and if you bring the pup straight back inside after he has performed, he will learn that if he gets on with things then he will be taken back into the warmth.

At first, the pup may not be able to hold his water all night. So make some allowance for this. If you have a crate, you can line the front of it with a newspaper, so your puppy does not have to soil his own bedding.

If you are not using a crate, you can put newspaper down for the pup overnight at some distance from his bed, or by a door. This practice has to be used with care, however, as it may give pup the idea that it is alright to wet in the night. Also, teaching him to regard a newspaper as something to perform on can have consequences should you inadvertently place the morning's paper on the floor...

A RESCUED DOG

If you have decided that you haven't the stamina for training a young pup, or maybe because of your age you feel that the dog could outlive you, you may have opted to take on a rescued, fully grown or adolescent Stafford. Make no mistake, most of the dogs that come to rescue have no bad habits. Fashion in dogs is just as fickle as fashion in clothes. But some have been allowed to develop bad habits – mainly through laziness on the part of their former owners – and are then 'dumped'. Fortunately, Staffords, unlike many other breeds, are very adaptable. Probably from their past history they seem to have the ability to change homes and to settle. It will help if you can find out something of the dog's background. Indeed, a good rescue group will try to match dog and owners. It would be very hard on say a six or seven-year-old Stafford brought up in the country in a one person household to be rehomed in a town in a family with

The Stafford is an adaptable dog and will soon learn to settle in a new home.

a large number of children.

If you are starting with an adult, I would still advise having a plan of how you are going to care for your dog, and what house rules you want him to abide by. You may find that you have to adapt some rules, or you may have to spend extra time getting the dog to adapt to life with you.

A friend of mine took on a retired guide dog for the blind who had been trained to perform only on grass, and she lived in a town house with a paved back yard. In desperation, she dug up part of this and laid grass! Actually, if you have the time, working on these little problems and solving them can be very interesting and rewarding, and you have the knowledge that you are giving a dog a second chance.

Caring for a Stafford

A Staffordshire Bull Terrier can live for 12 to 13 years, some longer. So caring for a Stafford is a big commitment. Of course, in return you will receive a great deal of love, many funny moments and a bucketful of anecdotes. Staffords are never dull or boring companions and, providing you have some sense of humour, once you have been owned by one you will never wish to be without the breed.

The early months of a Stafford's life require almost total commitment from yourself. These are the months when you will teach your Stafford most of the lessons he will need for life, and the more effort you put into these months the better reward you will receive in later years. His needs are both physical and mental, so we will start by dealing with the physical aspects.

CHOOSING A DIET

The most important consideration as far as daily care is concerned is how you are going to feed your Staffordshire Bull Terrier.

There are many diets that you can choose from. One of the priorities must be the ease of preparation and serving. This should not, however, be the only concern. The foremost question is to choose a diet which best suits your dog – and his requirements may well change over his lifetime. Not all diets suit all dogs. At the present time we have five dogs, and we serve three different diets.

Commerical diets

A ready-made commercial food can be either canned meat, plus biscuit, or a complete diet. Complete foods are extremely easy and clean to serve, but they are very high in protein so should be given in the exact amounts recommended by the manufacturers. Whenever you feed a commercial food – and there are dozens on the market – be wary of making additions. Commercial food producers have invested heavily in research in order to give the correct balance of ingredients. Additions may upset this balance and could cause problems for your dog. In extreme cases deformation of the limbs has occurred in dogs that have been fed too many additives.

If your dog is going through a rather dull, lethargic period in his life you perk him up' by a change of

Initially, your puppy may miss the competition of feeding with his littermates.

Natural food

You may choose to feed a fully 'natural' diet such as the BARF (Biologically Appropriate Raw Food) diet, which involves giving raw meat and bones. This is just as if the dog had killed an animal and eaten the whole thing – which in the wild is what he would do.

Alternatively you could buy meat from the butcher or dog meat, often sold in sausage form. To this you should add dog meal or biscuit. Feeding this type of food you must be sure that you are giving the dog all the minerals, carbohydrates and proteins that he needs. You may find you have to make additions such as calcium tablets or vitamins to his meal. You will need to do some homework on this to ensure you are giving the required amounts.

diet. It is not that the original diet is bad, but sometimes the mere act of giving him a change revitalises the dog.

Feeding regime

When your Stafford puppy first arrives home, he will need four meals a day. It will be to your advantage later in his life if you have not skimped on giving him top-quality food. We feed butcher's mince and terrier meal to our pups at this stage. We then introduce some canned puppy food with mixer going on to a junior type food as the pup grows older.

As your pup develops, he may well start to refuse or pick at one of his meals. This may be around the 10 to 11 week stage. After about 10 months he will probably be down to two meals, and after 18 months – the age where he will have completed most although not all of his growing – he could go down to

The Stafford is not a fussy feeder, and mealtimes will be a highspot of the day.

one meal a day. A Stafford is not fully mature, physically or mentally, until he is about four years of age.

A young puppy should have a good covering and feel quite chunky to the touch – there is time enough to harden him up when he is older. So don't be mean with the amount of food you are giving at this stage.

All your good work will come to nothing if you allow the pup to become infested with worms. A good breeder will have wormed the puppies two or three times before they leave for their new homes, and you will need to continue a worming programme (see Chapter Six: Health Care).

Mealtimes

The time you feed the dog is whatever fits in with your way of life. The only recommendation is that you don't feed him immediately before you feed yourself, in order to reinforce your superiority. In the wild the leader of the pack will eat first, and then the pecking order will go down until it reaches the most inferior. If you have more than one dog in the household you should feed them in this pecking order. Don't feel sorry for the under-dog and try to bring him up a peg or two by feeding him first; you could be building up trouble for him. We always put their bowls down in the

Ideal weight

The key to feeding an adult Stafford is to balance the amount of food with the amount of exercise he gets. In recent years in the show ring it has become increasingly popular to go for the 'stripped out look' in Staffords. This follows the fashionable look among our young women – the search for that magic size zero. Now if this look in a Stafford is obtained by giving the correct amount of food together with a lot of vigorous exercise, then all well and good, but too often it seems that this is achieved by restricting the intake of food. The tell-tale signs of this regime is a dull coat and a drawn look to the dog. A significant side effect of reducing the weight of a Stafford is that you tend to make him more active. Taken to extremes, the dog can become far too hyped up for comfortable living. In such cases it is

order of seniority – that is the order they have determined, not us. We usually feed our dogs separately, but if they are in the same room we never leave them unattended. We have seen too many cases where a dominant dog was cleaning his own bowl and then taking over the food of his less dominant partner. Moreover, if dogs are left unattended while eating it could result in a fight between competing dogs.

Bones and chews
Giving bones is a subject open for discussion. Most vets will tell you never to give them – they see problems from bones stuck in gullets or severe constipation due to the dog having too many bones. But there is nothing a dog enjoys more than a big knuckle-bone. If you are going to give bones they must be big and raw to prevent splintering. Be prepared for the fact that the first thing your

surprising how quickly an increase in weight can calm the dog down.

The other end of the spectrum is the problem of too much weight. This is rarely seen in the show ring, but is far too often evident in the world of pet dogs. The obese dog is ugly, and prone to injuries and other health problems. There is no doubt that carrying too much weight can shorten a dog's life. So don't let your Stafford become a couch potato in your efforts to get away from the coiled spring scenario – there is a happy medium.

The main reason that Staffords put on weight is that they are given too many titbits. So often we have been told: "he only gets half and pound of meat plus biscuit once a day". But on closer questioning it turns out that at coffee time he gets a biscuit, before he goes to bed he gets a rusk, etc. This is how the calories stack up. Giving a treat as a reward for good behaviour is an excellent idea. Many dogs learn the simple response to "Sit" from being given a biscuit – but keep the rewards small.

Stafford is likely to do on receiving this wonderful bone is to go out in the garden and bury it – but rest assured when it is nice and smelly he will dig it up and enjoy it all the more.

There are many types of chews now on the market – from narrow strips through to large pig's ears, and some that clean the dog's teeth. These products are very popular but must be used by the Stafford owner with some care. In no time at all the Stafford can reduce a chew to a mush which they sometimes try to swallow with awful results. I must say that I have never heard of a Stafford actually choking to death in this way, but I know of many instances when the owner has had to jump in and, with great difficulty, pull the offending object out of the dog's mouth. So be careful when giving any type of chew, and make sure that your Stafford is always supervised.

SOCIAL DEVELOPMENT

While you are caring for your puppy on a physical basis, you also need to be aware of his social development. The importance of socialising your

Make sure your Stafford is supervised if you give him a bone.

Stafford is dealt with in Chapter Five, but make sure you go out and about with your new puppy as soon as he has completed his inoculations.

As he grows older make sure your puppy spends some part of the day on his own. Learning that you can leave him but that you will return is a most important lesson – and the younger he learns it the better. Neighbours will complain if your dog sets up a howling routine every time you leave him.

All puppies chew, and as Staffords have such strong jaws they can do more damage than most other breeds. Damage limitation is definitely the best policy. Make sure your Stafford has safe toys, and if you have leave him for any length of time, tire him out first with a outing or a strenuous play session. Do not allow your puppy within easy reach of any valuable object – it is not fair to put temptation in his way.

If your Stafford is going through a chewing phase, this could be the time to use his crate with the door closed. Confining a puppy to a crate has prevented devastation for many owners. However, a crate should not be abused. If you go out to work it is simply not fair to keep a dog shut in a crate all day. You will need to arrange for a relative, friend or neighbour to let the dog out sometime during the day, so he can stretch his legs, relieve himself, and enjoy some human company.

A Stafford puppy needs to get used to spending some time on his own so he does not become anxious when you go out.

Kennel dogs

Staffords do not flourish as kennel dogs. Having kept boarding kennels for many years, we found we could reduce the weight of any of our Staffords simply by putting them in a kennel block for a week. The dogs were given the same amount of food, but they lost weight simply from pining.

The Stafford is a dog which needs human companionship. There have also been some very sad incidents of Staffords being stolen from outside kennels – even in small gardens close to the house. A Stafford's true character is never fully developed unless he is a member of a family.

HOLIDAYS

Of course, we all have to face the problem of what to do with our Staffords when we go on holiday. It is easier now to take dogs on holiday with us when going abroad. You must, however, plan well ahead so that you can get all the inoculations which may be demanded in the

It is a bonus if you can take your Stafford on holiday with you.

country you plan to visit. You should take time to check on any possible illness or dangerous pests that your dog might encounter there.

Otherwise the best solution is to find someone to care for your pet in his own home. You can hire a commercial house-sitter, but I would always take personal recommendations before making an arrangement. Alternatively you might find a relative or good friend who would be a foster parent for the required time. You will need to be sure that whoever you choose fully understands the character of Staffords in general, and your dog in particular.

If you can find a reputable boarding kennel – recommended by another Stafford owner if at all possible – then this is a reasonable alternative. You must make sure that the kennel owners like and understand Staffords and, as previously stated, be prepared for the fact that your Stafford may lose weight.

Beware of kennels where all the dogs are allowed to run together. This is unlikely to work out with a Stafford. If you feel you might need to kennel your dog any time throughout his life, get him accustomed to kennels when he is young. Putting an older dog into a large boarding kennel is purgatory for him; the noise and the bustle is very confusing for an old dog that has never ever experienced anything like it before. A young dog is much more adaptable, and, once settled into a familiar kennel, a Stafford can make a good boarder.

GROOMING

The Staffordshire Bull Terrier is a low maintenance breed and does not need extensive grooming to keep his coat in good order. A simple going over with a stiff brush will quickly rid him of dirt or loose hairs. It is a good idea to get into the routine of brushing your Stafford after a walk. We have a very dirty lane outside our house, so we keep a towel by the back door to wipe mucky feet and tummies, and then give a quick brush over.

Although the Stafford is a tough dog, he has almost no hair on his tummy, and therefore this part of his anatomy should be dried after walks in the wet. His feet will not come to any harm if left wet and muddy – but your kitchen floor will suffer.

You can also take this opportunity to check that there are no fleas or any signs of flea dirt in the coat. This is especially important if you have a cat, as fleas spread from cat to dog (See Chapter Six: Health Care for more information on external parasites).

Bathing

Your dog may need a bath from time to time. Most Staffords are quite fond of rolling in awful things that can smell overpowering!

You can bath your Stafford in the garden if it is fine, although I prefer to use the shower, protecting the plastic shower tray by spreading a thick layer of towels over the bottom. Use dog shampoo or baby shampoo, and soap him with care, making sure soapy water does not get into his eyes or down his ears. When he is well sudded, rinse with plenty of warm water. Hold a towel over him like an umbrella while he gives himself a really good shake. Then you can towel him down and he is ready to go.

If you are preparing your Stafford for a show, give him a bath a couple of days before the show rather than the

The Stafford is a low maintenance breed, and needs no more than regular brushing to keep his coat in good order.

After bathing, make sure your Stafford is dried thoroughly.

night before as bathing often brings up dandruff. This is unsightly on the dog's coat – especially if he is dark-coloured. Don't over bathe your dog as you reduce the oils in his coat and these serve as protection against the weather.

Regular checks

When you get into a routine of grooming your Stafford on a regular basis, you can take the opportunity to examine him. This will allow you to spot any problems at any early stage.

Teeth

Start by examining your Stafford's teeth. While he is young his gums will be very sore during teething time, so be very gentle with his mouth. It is still a good idea to check his mouth as

a Stafford can have what is termed 'converging' or 'in-growing' canines. This is where the large canine teeth on his bottom jaw are too far into the dog's mouth and do not clear the top ones. If this happens the canines can grow into the roof of the mouth.

Check when your puppy is losing his first teeth that the milk canines come out as the second ones come through. The second teeth might come up inside the baby ones, leaving the pup with two sets of these teeth. If you are concerned that this scenario is developing, consult your vet as he may decide to extract the milk teeth.

It is wise to clean your dog's teeth from an early age to prevent tooth decay later in his life. There are special dog toothpastes on the market which have flavours that are attractive to a dog. Alternatively you can buy chew-sticks which help to keep teeth clean.

Ears

Some Staffords suffer from ear problems, so it is a good idea to make sure your dog's ears are clean when you are giving him his 'once over'. If his ears smell mousey consult you vet. Early action is best to avoid a deep-seated problem. Never poke cotton buds down into the ear canal.

Nails

If your Stafford has the correct foot – that is halfway between the hare and

Regular brushing will keep the teeth clean and the gums healthy.

Nails can be kept in trim by using either a file or nail-clippers.

the cat foot – there should be no need to cut his nails. However, few dogs are blessed with the perfect foot, and a Stafford that has the long-toed, hare-type foot, will not wear his nails down, so they will need trimming. Walking on hard surfaces is essential – these act almost like a nail file. But if the problem is beyond this simple solution, there are a number of very good dog nail clippers on the market, or you could use a large nail file.

It will pay you to get your pup used to having his feet handled from the moment you bring him home. You don't have to do anything other than hold his paw, and look at his nails. This way, if you do have to cut his nails it will not be such a traumatic experience for him.

When you are cutting nails, put one arm firmly around him, lift his paw with the other hand and press lightly on his toes so that the nail is extended. This way you will be able to see where the quick of the nail begins. It is important that you avoid cutting into the quick as this will cause a great deal of bleeding. This is not dangerous but it is painful for the dog.

EXERCISING YOUR STAFFORD

The Stafford is a very active dog, but he does not need miles of walking every day. Until he is at least nine months of age he will need a very derate amount of exercise.

...eed, over-exercising at too early an age can harm his immature body. The main emphasis at this stage should be to introduce him to as many and as varied experiences as possible. Although Staffords should be very bold and not easily frightened when compared to other breeds it is still advisable to introduce him to the noises of the outside world as gently as possible. A short walk at this stage that takes him along a busy road is more use to him than two miles of walking through quiet country lanes. He must get used to being passed by cars, hearing heavy lorries change gear, meeting up with bicycles, push chairs and prams, as well as other dogs of course. If you live in the country you will have to make a special effort to get him in contact with all the noises of towns.

Perhaps taking him to a local open-air market is possible – certainly he will meet up with many different people there and all this will be a first-class learning curve for him. All dogs, but especially those that live in the country, should be introduced to livestock such as horses and cattle.

If you have to exercise your dog in a park, be sure to protect him from aggressive dogs. If you have the sort of Stafford that will not back down to the bully in the park, then be sensible and keep him on a lead near

A Stafford needs to learn how to behave around livestock.

For a Stafford, a game of retrieve combines physical exercise and mental stimulation, plus quality time interacting with his owner.

other dogs. No matter how much provocation you and your dog might have to endure, I can assure you that if your Stafford retaliates then he will always be blamed if a tussle ensues.

Fun and games

Because the Stafford is such an energetic, active dog, the very best sort of exercise for him is the violent type. The easiest way to provide this is to throw a ball. Make sure it is a good, hard ball and teach him to return it and give it up to you. This is a hard lesson for a Stafford to learn as his instinct is to keep hold of his 'trophy'. He may be desperate to have the ball thrown again and again, but he cannot seem to resist the temptation to run off every time you

want to take it from him. It may take some time for your dog to see the advantage of giving up his ball so that the game can continue, but the penny will drop in the end.

There is no better exercise for a Stafford than running, twisting, turning and generally playing rough and tumble with another Stafford. Care must be taken, however, to keep such games under control – they are certainly not to be encouraged with two male Staffords running together. If you have toys, such as a ball or a frisbee, be prepared to bring the game to a close if one of the dogs wants to keep all the toys for himself. A Stafford may be prepared to fight for the right to keep the toys, or he may

Clean up

It is incumbent upon all responsible dog owners to take a poop scooper, plastic bag or a nappy bag on walks in order to clean up after your dog. Nothing annoys the anti-dog lobby more than dogs fouling the public highways – and they are perfectly right to be outraged.

be challenged by the other dog.

Rough games between you and your Stafford may depend on how tough you are. A Stafford's heads is very hard if he barges your shins, and you will get a massive black eye if you are on the receiving end of a head-butt in the heat of the game. Personally, I prefer to throw balls or play with tug toys; I am not interested in wrestling as I believe it can send the wrong messages to a dog.

Pain Threshold

Staffords are notoriously tough and can keep going in spite of extreme illness or pain. It is important for the Stafford owner to be aware of this because of the danger of misinterpreting signs of ill health or injury.

A vet friend of ours had a Stafford taken to him two weeks after he had started acute diarrhoea. The dog was completely dehydrated by this time, had been walked a mile to the surgery. After being lifted on to the table he wagged his tail before collapsing and dying within a few minutes. We once took a dog who was 'limping a bit' to the vet, only to discover that both cruciate ligaments were ruptured. The vet said that had if it had been any other breed, the dog would have come into the surgery dragging his hind legs behind him.

Make sure you keep on good terms with a vet, especially one who appreciates the Stafford, so that you can consult him if you have any concerns about your dog's

We are lucky that the Stafford is an adaptable breed, and will cope with a change of circumstance.

health. Taking out pet insurance will give you peace of mind in case of unforeseen injury or the need for an expensive procedure.

CHANGING CIRCUMSTANCES
A Stafford likes routine and a stimulating but controlled way of life. Sometimes, however, life throws up the unexpected. For example, your family may be enlarged by the addition of an elderly relative. Although Staffords can be so effusive and exuberant with people, it is amazing how they can adapt their behaviour when faced with a

vulnerable older person.

The same can be said if a new baby comes into the family. However, the problem here is that we all try to protect a baby from a dog's germs – or what we perceive to be his germs. A dog should not be allowed to lick a child on the lips, but it is a good idea to let the dog have a really good sniff and lick baby's feet, for example. You can always wash them later.

If your dog has been the centre of your world and you then introduce a new baby into the family, make sure you spend plenty of time reassuring the dog that you still love him. Once

As your dog grows older, his needs will change.

he knows that this is so, and that the baby is just another member of the family, you will find he is protective of and very tolerant of it.

A cousin of mine cut his teeth on a Stafford's ear. When it got too much the dog simply jumped out of the way. Another family couldn't understand how their youngster was able to turn the tap on in the kitchen and, of course, leave it running. Eventually a bit of detective work uncovered the fact that the young child was persuading the Stafford to stand up against the sink and thus provide the child with a living stool for him to climb.

Never allow a child to exercise a fully-grown Stafford unsupervised. Staffords are very strong, and it could well be that a Stafford who is normally very tolerant of other dogs will have it in his mind that he should be protecting this small member of his family and thus get drawn into a fight with another dog.

THE OLDER STAFFORD
As your Stafford gets older, his care requirements will change.
If he is not taking as much exercise, he will not need the same volume of food. He may find it easier to cope with the same amount of food divided

into two meals, given morning and evening. If his digestion really starts to cause him problems, try changing his diet. There are commercial 'senior' diets on the market, which are easier to digest, or you could cook chicken and fish with rice for him. Many older Staffords suffer from arthritis and may need tablets or some form of additive to help their joints as they grow older.

If you take a young dog into the family, you may well find that the youngster gives your oldie a new lease of life. On the other hand, you must also guard against the old dog being ragged too much by the youngster.

LETTING GO

Inevitably the older dog will begin to fail. There are many medicines and procedures that vets can offer to prolong the life of an aging dog, which is fine as long as the dog has some quality of life. A dog that has been clean in the house all his life is distressed if he is unable to hold his water, and is fouling the house or may be even his bed. A dog that is unable to walk far or enjoy exploring his surroundings through infirmity, cannot seek comfort in the television as a human might.

In the end we have to ask ourselves (and be brutally honest): are we keeping this dog alive for his sake or for our own? It is a terrible decision to make but one that nearly all dog owners and dog lovers have had to make at some time.

If you decide that it is time to let go, you can make things easier by asking the vet to make a home visit. This is, of course, very expensive. If you choose to take the dog into the surgery, be brave and stay with him until the end. Stroking and talking to your dog as he slips away is the last act of kindness you can do for your dog.

You will know when the time has come to say goodbye to your beloved Stafford.

Educating your Stafford

A nyone who has ever spent time with a Stafford will be aware of the breed's excellent temperament and character. The Stafford is highly intelligent, inquisitive to the point of nosiness, versatile, courageous and enthusiastic about everything apart from a visit to the vet and – his most endearing quality – he possesses innate friendliness towards humans. Unfortunately, if mismanaged, these positive attributes can become negatives. More than ever before, Staffords need to be given opportunities to rise above the purpose for which they were originally bred while retaining both the positive characteristics of that inheritance and their versatility. Included throughout this chapter is relevant anecdotal evidence from personal observations of these dogs over a number of years.

EARLY SOCIALISATION

There are basically two things a dog needs to equip him for society and to enable him to enjoy a happy well-balanced life:

- Knowledge of his place and role within his family
- The ability to cope with the everyday situations he is likely to face during his lifetime.

The foundations for both of these are laid down from the time a puppy is born, but especially between the ages of four to ten weeks. This is known as the socialisation stage. Experiences and stimuli received during this time define the animal's future behaviour.

For the first 10 days of the newborn's life his eyes are still closed, and he is subjected to minimal stimulus other than the presence of his dam and littermates, warmth and food. Reputable Stafford breeders handle their newborn puppies, be it minimally, long before their eyes open. Initially they check them at birth for any congenital problems and gender identification then later to note markings and puppy conformation. This early hands-on activity is possibly the first step in pre-socialisation because the puppy will be aware of this new scent and recognise it with interest compared to the rest of his environment at a later stage.

The responsibility for sound socialisation also lies with the breeder because when this sensitive phase of learning begins, the puppy will still be with his dam.

A breeder will handle newborn puppies, which is the first step in pre-socialisation.

A Stafford puppy should meet a variety of people in calm, controlled circumstances.

MEETING PEOPLE

Research has shown that the earlier a puppy is introduced to humans the more confident he will be in their company. Puppies must have ongoing, non-excitable and regular contact with as many different people as possible. If there are no children in the family, the breeder needs to borrow some for supervised contact with the puppies.

Throughout their lives, a Stafford will come into contact with new people, including his owners, the vet, other dog owners at training club, and, if they are to be shown, judges, stewards and other exhibitors, so it is important that they are confident with people in every situation. It goes without saying that during the socialisation period, the human contact should be positive and non-threatening.

It is during this stage that some initial training can begin to prepare the puppy for the later handling he will receive. This can include gentle grooming, inspection of mouth, genital region, and the careful clipping of nail barbs. In addition to becoming people confident, the Stafford also

A puppy will soak up new experiences – both positive and negative – like a sponge.

needs to be confident with other animals he will be living with, so should be introduced to other species – most commonly cats – in the household. Again, this should be under supervision but with minimal interference, and if all goes well, maximum praise.

THE HOME ENVIRONMENT

In conjunction with socialisation, puppies need to be fully habituated. They need to become used to household items and sounds: the rustle of a bin liner being shaken out can be a startling experience to a youngster. The puppy needs to be accustomed to the sound of the television, washing machine, vacuum cleaner and computer games, if he is to be comfortable with, and equipped for, his place in life. If the litter is housed away from the main bustle of the home, pre-recordings of household noises can be introduced as a matter of course.

NEGATIVE EXPERIENCES

Despite the very best intentions and a well-balanced programme of

A Stafford needs to learn how to meet and greet other dogs.

socialisation, puppies do carry negative experiences with them from this sensitive stage. Polly, the foundation bitch of my breed line, had two particular dislikes that continued throughout her life: cushions and ham. She was bred and socialised by a family with children, the youngest of which (I noticed when I collected Polly at 10 weeks) protected his little legs from the onslaught of her sharp puppy teeth by pushing her away with the nearest cushion. She was never actually alarmed by the presence of a cushion, but always viewed it as a frustrating enemy and as a result would savage it. When I arrived to collect her I was told that both she and her mother had been on a raiding mission. One of the children had left the fridge door ajar, and Mum and daughter had consumed a large quantity of fresh ham. Post-raid mayhem, vomiting dogs and crying children had been sufficient to leave a negative association in Polly's mind and from then on she never ate ham.

The most obvious problem associated with the socialisation stage is that after about 10 weeks a puppy will be fearful of anything it has not previously encountered, and as many puppies do not leave their litters until eight weeks – although the ideal age would be six to seven weeks – the new owners have very little time to address shortfalls in learning.

There are many problems resulting from poor or under-socialisation and habituation that stay with the animals throughout their lives and are difficult (if not impossible) to address at a later stage. Below are a few common ones and likely reasons for these in the Stafford:

If a Stafford is well socialised, he will not feel threatened and will respond in a positive manner.

- **Stafford is reluctant to have its feet touched.**
  Negative experience with nail clippers too close to the quick or never had its paws inspected.
- **Stafford not comfortable with its own species.**
  Orphaned puppy with no canine contact.
- **Stafford is boistrous with visitors and jumps up to greet them.**
  Over enthusiastic greeting by strangers. (During socialisation it is important that the puppy's excitement is allowed to calm before a stranger fusses it). Very difficult to achieve!
- **Stafford uncomfortable around traffic.**
  Was reared in a quiet or rural location with minimal exposure to the sound of traffic.
- **Mouthing owner's/visitor's arms.**

New owner failed to continue the natural training begun by the dam and littermates who cry out if bitten too hard. This training must be continued until the puppy is 4-5 months.
- **Stafford is wary of the new baby.**
  Not exposed to baby sounds – or young children. Reared in an adult only environment.

SOCIALISING WITH OTHER DOGS

It must never be forgotten that the Staffordshire Bull Terrier was originally bred as a fighting dog. Fighting was made illegal but the Stafford survived because of his wonderful temperament and personality. The Stafford's specific function has become obsolete but negative association lives on and we must continue to concentrate on developing the image of the breed so

A Stafford that has been socialised throughout his puppy and juvenile stages will adapt readily to new situations.

that the Stafford is viewed by others as we view him ourselves.

While we Stafford lovers imagine that our unique dogs were beamed down from the planet 'joyous', they are – like all dogs – descendents of the wolf. As such they have inherited the genetic make-up of a true pack living animal that survived because of clearly defined hierarchies. This inheritance is the foundation we build on for a peaceable future with our dogs.

Later in this chapter we will look more closely at the qualities a Stafford would like in his owner – or in this context pack leader – but there are activities that can be undertaken during the socialisation stage which help prepare your Stafford for a non-aggressive future with regard to his interaction with other breeds.

In a variety of different situations I have seen the same scenario: a flustered Stafford owner tugging his snarling charge away from another dog – and the owner always says the same thing. "He's fine with my Staffs, he just hates other breeds." He probably does not, or did not previously, hate all other breeds, but was not exposed to them or had a bad experience with them during the socialisation stage.

In an ideal world every Stafford would live in a multi-dog breed environment for the first three months of his life so that he receives maximum exposure to every form of canine – but clearly this is not feasible. Therefore we, as owners, must try to replicate as much of this dream situation as possible.

The following suggests "do's" and "don't's" during the socialisation stage of a Stafford.

Do:

- Attend puppy socialisation classes, especially if your puppy left his dam and siblings at an early age.
- Let your puppy socialise with other (vaccinated) dogs, but ensure your pup and the other dog(s) are on leads and supervised.
- Praise all positive interaction with other dogs.
- Try to expose your puppy to different ages, sizes and breeds of dogs.
- Ensure that exposure to other dogs is ongoing.

Don't:

- Scoop your Stafford into your arms out of the way of a big dog's

friendly, if overpowering, welcome. It will make the puppy fearful.

- Let your puppy off the lead with dogs you are unsure of.
- Introduce your pup to other dogs in their territory. Always choose somewhere away from beds or toys.

ON-GOING SOCIALISATION

No matter how well our Staffords are socialised, if they do not continue to receive socialisation during their juvenile stage – which is from three months to when they become adults – then they will regress.

There is no excuse for anyone to neglect the reinforcement of the learning and experiences that most breeders have actively set out to equip their puppies with. A little time set aside everyday for fuss, grooming and general companionship will ensure a Stafford that is eager to

Puppies need to learn what is considered acceptable. A pup who is used to nipping his littermates must be taught to curb this behaviour.

please and willing to build on his experiences.

A breeder that I know sent a fully socialised Staffie bitch puppy abroad, only to learn later that the puppy had been left day after day in a kennel environment with little contact with the new owner or kennel staff. At six months when she was ready to be shown, she was so withdrawn and nervous that she was sold on. Fortunately, she went to a family home where she was sympathetically treated.

Scientific research has proven conclusively that what occurs (or does not occur) during the sensitive stage of socialisation (4-10 week), and the juvenile stage (12 weeks to adulthood) has a direct bearing on future behaviour. However, the individual character, inherited traits and personality of each animal needs to be taken into account because how a dog perceives experiences, and his learning as a result of these experiences, may differ.

TRAINING THE STAFFORD

The characteristics in a Stafford – intelligence, eagerness to please and versatility – should make him an ideal candidate for training. He loves people but unfortunately this eagerness to be

These are the benefits

Training your Staffordshire Bull Terrier has many benefits, including:

- Emphasising the role of the owner in the household as the pack leader: The wolf terminology.
- Building a closer bond with the animal: Shared communication.
- Clearly defining hierarchies: You are training the animal therefore you are in charge – it is a lesser pack member.
- Mind stimulation: Staffords love learning new activities and being rewarded by praise and encouragement and – preferably in addition – food.

friends with everyone can be one of the biggest barriers to learning. How can a Stafford concentrate on one person telling him to "Stay" when there is a house full of other people who want to make a fuss of him? How can he listen to his owner telling him to be "Steady" on the lead when the street is full of people he must meet and greet?

Anyone who has taken a well-socialised Stafford puppy out in public for the first time will recognise the description of a little creature (tail wagging to distraction) looking up at every approaching person in the expectation that attention will be forthcoming. If it is not, there is a slight lull in the tail wagging until the next person comes into view and the process is repeated.

The aim is for your Stafford to walk on a loose lead without pulling.

A Stafford puppy wriggling with glee is hard to resist, which is why it is important that the basics are learned in a more controlled situation before the big debut for the rest of the world.

Rule number one for training therefore is to ensure initial commands are learned in a suitably quiet and people free area where the puppy can concentrate on the learning process without distraction.

Other considerations should be:

• The time of day. If the puppy has run around all day he may be too tired for effective learning.

• When he had his last meal. Puppies with full stomachs are less likely to respond to treats (if treats are to be given) and will want to sleep rather than train.

• The mood of the trainer. If you have had a fractious day at work this may well affect your patience levels with a puppy during his training session.

Wearing a collar

Puppies are usually introduced to their first collar at about eight weeks old. First collars should be reasonably soft and easy to put on and remove. An owner fumbling with a stiff new buckle while the puppy is in effect

Verbal communication

Prior to introducing commands or cues for exercises, you will need to decide what the puppy should be taught. You must also ensure that other members of the household are aware of, and use, the same commands for the desired response. It is counter productive if one family member says "Come" and the other says "Here" when they want the dog's attention. Again, the fact that all the family members are able to issue commands which the dog responds to, emphasises the pack hierarchy.

There are basic commands or cues that every dog should know and should respond to. These are:
• Come
• Stay

trapped in their grasp is not the ideal way to introduce a puppy to training equipment. If the puppy has already been taught to sit then it is a good idea to ask him to sit while the collar is put on. The collar should only be left on for about 10 minutes the first time. The puppy will roll around and generally scratch at this alien item trying to remove it. Gradually increase the wearing time until the pup becomes accustomed to it. Once he is totally comfortable with his collar, lead training – with a lightweight lead – can begin.

Lead training
For all of his little life to date the puppy has been a free spirit, now all of a sudden he finds himself restrained. It is therefore important that he learns the benefit of the lead – being on the lead means he is close to his owner. Having lead trained

- No
- Leave
- Wait
- Sit

There are additional cues that are likely to be needed when training Staffords:
- Steady (as in slow down)
- Off (the furniture)
- Bed (when your Stafford still wants to play at midnight!)

It is important that the dog's name is said before each cue. There are two reasons for this:
- If the dog is in a multi-dog household then all will come running (or should do) if the "Come" command is used and the name not specified.
- Using the name alerts the dog and grabs his attention as he knows a command will follow.

many puppies over a number of years, I have found that the first step once the lead is attached to the collar is to encourage the puppy to you and make a big fuss of him. Pick up the lead and step back until puppy is at the end of the lead and can just feel the pressure, then call him to you for fuss. Repeat until you are sure that the puppy is comfortable with you being at the far end of his lead, knowing he can access you easily.

This exercise is sufficient for a first collar and lead experience. Repeat over the next couple of days but gradually try a gentle pull of the lead, encouraging the puppy towards you. The puppy should be happy to respond as he does not see the lead as a threat to his freedom but as a means to come close to you – and there is nowhere else he would rather be. If you sense, or your puppy displays, reluctance, revert to your

will never learn anything – he will have fallen asleep before he hears the command that follows his name! Stafford owners are top of the 'sensible names for dogs' league. The breed abounds with Bens, Mollys and Billys – short punchy names that are easy to learn and respond to.

You can reward your Stafford with a treat when he responds to the "Sit" command.

original tack and call him over for fuss. Gentle perseverance and patience will ensure a happy puppy that is eager to trot on the lead beside you.

The first formal walk on the lead should be up and down the garden where he already feels safe and he can explore under your guidance. If you do sense a reluctance to walk freely beside you, redirect his attention to something else (some rustling leaves, for example) so that he experiences that being together on a lead with his owner is fun.

Name game

Anyone who decides they want to train their dog should think wisely about the name they choose. A dog who has been named Fred-Fitzherbert

The "Come" and the "Sit" commands

Logically, the "Come" command should be the one that the Stafford puppy learns first. It is an easy command to respond to because Staffords do not need a particular reason to go to someone for fuss. The owner's response to the pup when he is called should be given encouragingly, but without excess excitement as Staffords can become over enthusiastic in their greeting. It is important to ensure that the pup – the future dog – can be called in for a purpose, not necessarily for an excited greeting. It is therefore worth teaching the pup the "Sit" command prior to "Come".

Teaching "Sit" is easy. You can simply watch the behaviour of a puppy and say '"Sit" at the exact moment he sits down naturally – then reward him with praise. This will soon set up an association if repeated often and accurately enough. The puppy will sit when he hears the word.

Alternatively, when the puppy is in a quiet and receptive mood, spend quality training time with him. Say firmly: "Billy, Sit", and press his rear end gently down into the sitting position. Reward then repeat until the puppy is doing this to command. Do not prolong the "Sit" sessions, but do repeat them often so that they become a natural thing to do at any time of the day.

Returning to the "Come" command, the trainer now has something to ask of the puppy when he has been asked to "Come' rather than just expecting a fuss. The basic technique is "Billy, come" at which point Billy trots over expectantly. Give an encouraging pat or "good boy" then say: "Billy, sit". If Billy sits then much praise should be given. If Billy does not because he was confused by the linkage of two commands then try and concentrate on the "Come" – increase the fuss when he responds, but then ask him to "Sit".

Bear in mind with a Stafford, you bestow the reward, he should not expect to take it. A Stafford demanding fuss will jump up in his eagerness to have more, and if you respond you are acting out of the character of a pack leader. Pack leaders give their approval sparingly and when they see fit, not when their subordinates ask for it.

If the pup will not come because he perceives there is something more interesting to do, then re-start

Make yourself sound exciting so your Stafford wants to come to you.

training using a loose lead. Use the 'Billy, come' cue, and gently tug the lead encouraging the puppy towards you. This generally spurs the puppy into action and he will lollop over happily. Give praise.

Never pull the puppy towards you. This is bullying by using your strength over his. He will recognise this and will pull against you. Persist with the voice command technique. Staffords

Build up the Stay exercise in easy stages, gradually increasing the distance you can leave your Stafford.

are intelligent and reward in the form of praise will always win them over.

Teaching "Stay"

Once the puppy has mastered "Come" and "Sit", then "Stay" will follow naturally and with the minimum of additional training – we hope!

The puppy has already been alerted to being called over and because he knows you are likely to ask him to "Sit", he will naturally be calmer and more responsive than if he was dancing around in the excitement at being called to you for fuss. Say: "Billy, stay" and take a couple of backward steps. The dog has one of two options: option one – he will follow or, preferably, option two – he will sit in amazement for a short while wondering why you should possibly want to step away from him. At this point, call him over and praise him before he has the chance to change his mind and follow you.

The psychological difference in the puppy's mind is that in option one you are curtailing what he naturally wants to do – follow you – (which he perceives as negative), but in option two you are bestowing a reward (praise) before he had actually taken a decision. Therefore it feels he has somehow caused the reward – a positive – to happen.

Repeat the exercise and, when you catch the puppy's eye, you will notice his little chest puffed up with controlled excitement. He knows he can expect praise, but he will wait in order to savour the moment.

Do not ever widen the distance between yourself and the puppy until you are satisfied that he will stay at a short distance, and never expect him to stay for long periods until he has completely mastered the command, otherwise he will become bored and roll around amusing himself.

Returning to option one, the puppy that follows when told to stay. Repeat the command and if he still follows, remain close enough to be able to put your arm out and hold the puppy in the same position. Repeat 'Billy, stay' and gradually move backwards releasing your hold. There will be pouts but ensure his interest – rather than the pouting – is encouraged and once again, try and pre-empt the moment he decides to follow by much praise for the fact that he did stay for a while.

Teaching "No" and "Leave"

The Stafford equivalent of the word "No" can be seen in the nursing bitch when a sharp nailed, biting pup has overstepped the mark once too often on her over-suckled teats. It is effective and commands an instant cessation of the undesired activity, or it prevents an activity that is about to occur.

If "No" is used too often its impact is reduced. "No" should not mean: "you can't have that bone" nor should it mean: "stop mugging the visitors". "No" should be high impact.

The Stafford does not need to be given a reason for the "No" command but should instantly obey it. Tone of voice and the owner's natural body language in a "No" situation (generally thrust towards the puppy) evokes the response.

On other occasions, the "Leave" command can be used. "Leave" the bone (for the moment). "Leave" the toy (for later). Leave does not threaten nor suggest dire outcomes;

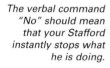

The verbal command "No" should mean that your Stafford instantly stops what he is doing.

Teach your dog to give up his toy on request.

it is a command to be obeyed like "Sit" and "Come" but it is part of the everyday communication between owner and Stafford.

"Leave" can be taught at an early age, but there does need to be a reward – a swap –for obedience. Returning to the wolf pack, imagine a newly weaned cub finding a sliver of meat left from the pack's feeding frenzy. The cub is not going to give up his prize easily. He will guard his morsel to the best of his capability. He will only be encouraged to part with it if there is a good game to be had with his siblings, a bigger slice of the kill from his mother, or the promise of a well-earned sleep. Therefore, when teaching "Leave", offer praise and fuss for what has been relinquished, or a treat or walk as a swap until the command is learned and becomes second nature, and is a willingly obeyed command.

Teaching "Wait"

In my experience, "Wait" is most easily learned by a Stafford when it is combined with other activities, such as playing in the garden. There the "Wait" command can be given before a toy is thrown and the puppy has to stand in anticipation of the throw. "Wait" is used to command the puppy to stand still while a garden gate is being opened before going out for a walk, and "Wait" is said before crossing a busy road. "Wait" as a command can be used to control (generally), more so than any other command, because it is logical. It indicates to the dog that nothing will occur unless the command is obeyed: the toy will not be thrown, the gate will not be opened, we will not cross the road. 'Wait' to a Stafford means: "wait for something to follow."

OPPORTUNITIES FOR STAFFORDS

The Staffordshire Bull Terrier is an intelligent dog who will enjoy being given an outlet for his energy – both mentally and physically.

Exhibiting in the show ring

For owners of a pedigree Stafford who may have an interest in showing there are training clubs throughout the country that hold regular (usually weekly) ringcraft training sessions to help prepare.

The ideal Stafford owner

Consistency in commands and rewards combined with clear firm verbal communication should be what we all aim for when training our puppies. As mentioned previously, ensure that the command or cue words are adhered to – especially at the basic training stage – and that one word communicates to the puppy the action that is required.

Dogs recognise and respond to body language: a disinterested, lethargic posture will transmit instantly, as will one bristling with impatience. Therefore it is important that we are always motivated and able to encourage sustainable learning in our dogs. Encouragement and understanding should go hand in hand. We all have off days – so do our animals – but we must be aware of this and ensure that each session ends on a positive note. Exasperation must not take over from reason, nor should we be disappointed at our puppy's lack of goal attainment. We may not have achieved as much as we had hoped but we still have that bond of understanding and communication and we can build on that another day.

All breed canine ringcraft clubs

In addition to being examined by a judge, learning to stand and move correctly, these clubs also include a wide range of socialisation activities. A Stafford attending ringcraft can expect an exercise such as 'weaving', where dogs and owners stand in a large circle and each dog takes turns to 'weave' around all the other dogs with minimal investigation. Or you and your dog may stand opposite another dog and his owner, walking towards them and crossing to the other side. Such activities promote positive interaction with other breeds.

Traditional Stafford breed clubs

Training sessions tend to focus more fully on the specifics of Stafford presentation so the evening will consist of a number of 'classes' in which dogs are familiarised with being gone over by the judge, will be asked to move and then placed in a final line-up. An advantage of breed specific clubs is that they are usually run by experienced Stafford owners who have a wealth of knowledge of the breed to pass on to novice handlers.

Good Citizen Scheme

This scheme consists of three levels of award – bronze, silver and gold – that an interested Stafford and its owner can work towards achieving.

Prior to these, the Puppy Foundation Assessment (for puppies up to a maximum of 12 months) aims to provide a means of socialising (by attendance at courses) and to lay down a foundation for education and training.

All awards require the dog to successfully undertake a specified range of different exercises.

- Bronze Award: Providing handlers with basic knowledge of understanding and training their dog.
- Silver Award: As bronze, but good knowledge is the aim.
- Gold Award: A greater knowledge of understanding and training.

The bronze award covers exercises such as walking on the lead without distractions and grooming without a struggle.

Gold level includes sending the dog to bed and staying down in one place.

Agility

When looking at a mature Stafford standing foursquare, the term 'aerodynamic' does not instantly spring to mind. Yet Staffords are

The Staffordshire Bull Terrier is built on athletic lines and responds well to the challenge of agility.

remarkably agile and fast when free-ranging. My young dog loves to race and can turn on a sixpence if called back mid gallop. If there's a stream or a wall in his path (all the better), he will clear both with yards to spare and not miss a stride on landing.

For the more active Stafford owner, agility is fun and ideal for the mental and physical well-being of the dog. Staffords have much stamina, are strong, and well suited to obstacles such as hurdles, brush fences, spread jumps and hoops. Competitive agility is based on the height of dog: large, medium and small and the fences and obstacles take into account these heights.

Training should always be reward-based and positive.

Staffords doing what they are best at

There are many people who have no access to animals. They may be in residential care homes, special needs schools or hospices where keeping animals cannot be allowed. It is well reported that animals can have a therapeutic effect on people but these people do not have the opportunity to experience this unless the animals can be taken to them. Pets As Therapy aims to provide people with this experience and welcomes appropriate dogs,

who are temperamentally assessed and must be vaccinated. The only requirement on visits is that the dog is kept on a loose lead and is under control at all times.

The breed standard for the Staffordshire Bull Terrier includes "........highly intelligent and affectionate, especially with children"

For those owners who have a desire to share the virtues of this lovely breed, what better way than allowing him to show his affection for the benefit of others?

Health care for Staffords

S taffordshire Bull Terriers are stoical dogs with a good life-span, which can run well into double figures provided their needs are met. As well as many of the terrier traits one would expect, the Stafford is renowned as a plucky, faithful companion, a willing friend on a non-conditional basis. He will, however, of necessity rely on you for food and shelter, accident prevention and medication. A healthy Stafford is a happy chap.

There are a few significant genetic conditions which have been recognised in the Stafford. They will be covered in depth later in the chapter.

ROUTINE HEALTH CARE

Vaccination

There is much debate over the issue of vaccination at the moment. Timing of the final part of the initial vaccination course for a puppy and the frequency of subsequent booster vaccinations are both under scrutiny. An evaluation of the relative risk for each disease plays a part, depending on the local situation.

Many owners think that the actual vaccination is the protection, so that their puppy can go out for walks as soon as he or she has had the final part of the puppy vaccination course. This is not the case.

The rationale behind vaccination is to stimulate the immune system into producing protective antibodies which will be triggered if the patient is subsequently exposed to that particular disease. This means that a further one or two weeks will have to pass before an effective level of protection will have developed. Vaccines against viruses stimulate longer lasting protection than those against bacteria, whose effect may only persist for a matter of months in some cases. There is also the possibility of an individual failing to mount a full immune response to a vaccination: although the vaccine schedule may have been followed as recommended, that particular dog remains vulnerable.

An individual's level of protection against rabies, as demonstrated by

The timing of vaccinations depends on the incidence of disease in the area.

A visit to the vet for a booster injection can be used to give your Stafford a routine health check.

the antibody titre in a blood sample, is routinely tested in the UK in order to fulfil the requirements of the Pet Travel Scheme (PETS). This is not required at the current time with any other individual diseases in order to gauge the need for booster vaccination or to determine the effect of a course of vaccines. Instead, your veterinary surgeon will advise a protocol based upon the vaccines available, local disease prevalence, and the lifestyle of you and your dog. It is worth remembering that

maintaining a fully effective level of immune protection against the disease appropriate to your locale is vital. These are serious diseases which may result in the demise of your dog, and some may have the potential to be passed on to his human family (so-called zoonotic potential for transmission). This is where you will be grateful for your veterinary surgeon's own knowledge and advice.

The American Animal Hospital Association laid down guidance at the end of 2006 for the vaccination of dogs in North America. Core diseases were defined as distemper, adenovirus, parvovirus and rabies. So-called non-core diseases are kennel cough, Lyme disease and leptospirosis; a decision to vaccinate against one or more non-core diseases will be based on an individual's level of risk, determined on life-style and where you live in the US.

Do remember, however, that the booster visit to the veterinary surgery is not 'just' for a booster. I am regularly correcting my clients when they announce that they have 'just' brought their pet for a booster. Instead, this appointment is a chance for a full health check and evaluation of how a particular dog is doing. After all, we are all conversant with the adage that a human year is

Distemper

Also called 'hardpad' from the characteristic changes to the pads of the paws. It has a worldwide distribution, but fortunately vaccination has been very effective at reducing its occurrence. It is caused by a virus and affects the respiratory, gastro-intestinal (gut) and nervous systems, so it results in a wide range of illnesses. Fox and urban stray dog populations are most at risk, and therefore responsible for local outbreaks.

equivalent to seven canine years. There have been attempts in recent times to re-set the scale for two reasons: small breeds live longer than giant breeds, and dogs are living longer than previously. I have seen dogs of seventeen and eighteen years of age but to say a dog is '119' or '126' years old is plainly meaningless. It does emphasise the fact, though, that a dog's health can change dramatically over the course of a single year because dogs age at a far greater rate than humans.

For me, as a veterinary surgeon, the booster vaccination visit is a challenge: how much can I find of which the owner was unaware, such as rotten teeth or a heart murmur? Even monitoring bodyweight year upon year is of use because bodyweight can creep up, or down, without an owner realising. Being overweight is unhealthy, but it may take an outsider's remark to make an owner realise that there is a problem. Conversely, a drop in bodyweight may be the only pointer to an underlying problem.

The diseases against which dogs can be vaccinated include:

Adenovirus

Canine Adenovirus 1 (CAV-1) affects the liver (hepatitis) and the classic 'blue eye' appearance in some affected dogs, whilst CAV-2 is a cause of kennel cough (see later). Vaccines often include both canine adenoviruses.

Kennel cough is highly contagious and spreads rapidly among dogs that live together.

Kennel cough

Also known as infectious tracheobronchitis, *Bordetella bronchiseptica* is not only a major cause of kennel cough but also a common secondary infection on top of another cause. Being a bacterium, it is susceptible to treatment with appropriate antibiotics, but the immunity stimulated by the vaccine is therefore short-lived (six to twelve months).

This vaccine is often in a form administered down the nostrils in order to stimulate local immunity at the point of entry, so to speak. Do not be alarmed to see your veterinary surgeon using needle and syringe to draw up the vaccine because the needle will be replaced with a special plastic introducer, allowing the vaccine to be gently instilled into each

nostril. Dogs generally resent being held for the vaccine to be administered more than the actual intra-nasal vaccine, and I have learnt that covering the patient's eyes helps greatly.

Kennel cough is, however, rather a catch-all term for any cough spreading within a dog population – not just in kennels, but also between dogs at a training session or breed show, or even mixing out in the park. Many of these infections may not be *B. bronchiseptica* but other viruses, for which one can only treat symptomatically. Parainfluenza virus is often included in a vaccine programme because it is a common viral cause of kennel cough. Kennel cough can seem alarming. There is a persistent cough accompanied by production of white

Lyme disease is still a rare occurrence in the UK.

frothy spittle which can last for several weeks, during which time the patient is highly infectious to other dogs. I remember when it ran through our five Border Collies – there were white patches of froth on the floor wherever you looked!

Other features of Kennel Cough include sneezing, a runny nose, and conjunctivitis. Fortunately, these infections are generally self-limiting, most dogs recovering without any long-lasting problems, but an elderly dog may be knocked sideways by it, akin to the effects of a common cold on a frail elderly person.

Lyme disease

This is a bacterial infection transmitted by hard ticks. It is therefore found in those specific areas of the US where ticks are found such as north-eastern states, some southern states, California and the upper Mississippi region. It does also occur in the UK but at a low level, so vaccination is not routinely offered.

Clinical disease is manifested primarily as limping due to arthritis, but other organs affected include the heart, kidneys and nervous system. It is readily treatable with appropriate antibiotics, once diagnosed, but the causal bacterium, *Borrelia burgdorferi,* is not cleared from the body totally and will persist.

Prevention requires both vaccination and tick control, especially as there are other diseases transmitted by ticks. Ticks carrying *B. burgdorfer*i will transmit it to humans as well, but an infected dog cannot pass it to a human.

Leptospirosis

Disease is caused by *Leptospira interogans*, a spiral-shaped bacterium. There are several natural variants or serovars. Each is characteristically found in one or more particular host animal species which then acts as a reservoir, intermittently shedding leptospires in the urine. Infection can also be picked up at mating, via bite wounds, across the placenta, or through eating the carcases of infected animals such as rats.

A serovar will cause actual clinical disease in an individual when two conditions are fulfilled: the individual is not the natural host species, and is also not immune to that particular serovar. Leptospirosis is a zoonotic disease, known as Weil's disease in humans, with implications for all those in contact with an affected dog. It is also commonly called rat jaundice, reflecting the rat's important role as a reservoir of *Leptospira icterohaemorrhagiae* to both humans and dogs. The UK National Rodent Survey 2003 found a wild brown rat population of 60 million, equivalent at the time to one rat per person. There is as much a risk for the Stafford living with a family in a town as the Stafford leading a rural lifestyle. Signs of illness reflect the organs affected by a particular serovar. In man, there may be a 'flu-like symptoms or a more serious, sometimes life-threatening disorder involving major body organs.

The illness in a susceptible dog may be mild, the dog recovering within two to three weeks without treatment but going on to develop long-term liver or kidney disease. In contrast, peracute illness may result in a rapid deterioration and death following initial malaise and fever. There may also be anorexia, vomiting, diarrhoea, abdominal pain, joint pain, increased thirst and rate of urination, jaundice, and ocular changes. Haemorrhage is a common feature because of low platelet numbers, manifesting as bleeding under the skin, nose-bleeds (epistaxis), and the presence of blood in the urine and faeces (haematuria and melaena respectively).

Treatment requires rigorous intra-venous fluid therapy to support the kidneys. Being a bacterial infection, it is possible to treat leptospirosis with specific antibiotics, although a prolonged course of several weeks is needed in order to avoid the development of the chronic carrier state. Strict hygiene and barrier nursing are needed in order to avoid onward transmission of leptospirosis.

Vaccination reduces the severity of disease, but cannot prevent the development of chronic carrier state following exposure. There is little or no cross-protection between serovars. This means that vaccination will result in protection against only those serovars included in that particular vaccination. In the UK, vaccines have classically included *L icterohaemorrhagiae* (rat-adapted serovar) and *L canicola* (dog-specific serovar). The latter is of special significance to us humans, since disease will not be apparent in an infected dog but leptospires will be shed intermittently. The situation in the US is less clear-cut. Blanket vaccination against leptospirosis is not considered necessary because it only occurs in certain areas. There has also been a shift in the serovars implicated in clinical disease, reflecting the effectiveness of vaccination and the migration of wildlife reservoirs carrying different serovars from rural areas, so you must be guided by your veterinarian's knowledge of the local situation.

Canine Parvovirus (CPV)

Canine Parvovirus disease first appeared in the late 1970s when it was feared that the UK's dog population would be decimated by it because of the lack of immunity in the general canine population. This was a notion which terrified me at the time, but which did not happen on the scale envisaged.

There are two forms of the virus (CPV-1, CPV-2) affecting domesticated dogs. CPV-2 also affects wild dogs. The virus is highly contagious, picked up via the mouth/nose from infected faeces. The incubation period is about five days.

CPV-2 causes two types of illness: gastro-enteritis (vomiting, haemorrhagic diarrhoea, fever) and heart disease in puppies born to unvaccinated dams (myocarditis or inflammation of the cardiac muscle, heart failure, respiratory distress, diarrhoea), both of which often result in death.

Infection of puppies less than three weeks of age with CPV-1 manifests as diarrhoea, vomiting, difficulty breathing, and fading puppy syndrome. CPV-1 can cause abortion and fetal abnormalities in breeding bitches.

There is no specific treatment, the mainstay being aggressive fluid therapy coupled with anti-emetic drugs to counteract vomiting, and antibiotic cover because of the marked reduction in white blood cell numbers caused by the virus. In the convalescent period, an easily digested diet is essential, with low fibre content, whilst the lining of the

Young puppies are especially vulnerable to Canine Parvovirus.

Rabies

This is another zoonotic disease and there are very strict control measures in place. Vaccines were once only available in the UK on an individual basis for dogs being taken abroad. Pets travelling into the UK had to serve six months compulsory quarantine so that any pet incubating rabies would be identified before release back into the general population. Under the Pet Travel Scheme, provided certain criteria are met (and I would refer you to the DEFRA website for up-to-date information – www.defra.gov.uk) then dogs can re-enter the UK without being quarantined.

Dogs to be imported into the US have to show that they were vaccinated against rabies at least thirty days previously; otherwise, they have to serve effective internal quarantine for thirty days from the date of vaccination against rabies, in order to ensure they are not incubating it. An exception is made for dogs entering from countries recognised as being rabies-free, in which case it has to be proved that they lived in that country for at least six months beforehand.

gastro-intestinal tract recovers. The virus is able to survive for several months in the environment. Although resistant to most disinfectants, it is susceptible to sodium hypochlorite at a dilution rate of 1:30 bleach:water.

Occurrence is mainly low now, thanks to vaccination against CPV-2. There is no vaccine available for CPV-1. The disease is more often mild or sub-clinical, with recovery more likely, although a recent outbreak in my area did claim the lives of several puppies and dogs. It is also occasionally seen in the elderly unvaccinated dog.

PARASITES

A parasite is defined as an organism deriving benefit on a one-way basis from another, the host. It goes without saying that it is not to the parasite's advantage to harm the host to such an extent that the benefit is lost, especially if it results in the death of the host. This means a dog could harbour parasites, internal and/or external, without there being any signs apparent to the owner. Many canine parasites can, however, transfer to humans with variable consequences, so routine preventative treatment is advised against particular parasites. Just as with vaccination, risk assessment plays a part – for example, there is no need for routine heartworm treatment in the UK (at present), but it is vital in the US and in Mediterranean countries.

A preventative worming programme is essential as a dog with internal parasites can pose a threat to human health.

Tapeworms (Cestodes)

The primary source of the commonest tapeworm species (*Dipylidium caninum*) will be fleas and lice which can carry the eggs as intermediate hosts. Most multi-wormers will be active against these tapeworms. They are not a hazard to human health but it is not pleasant to see the wriggly rice grain tapeworm segments emerging from your dog's back passage whilst he is lying in front of the fire.

A tapeworm of significance to human health is *Echinococcus granulosus*, found in a few parts of the UK, mainly in Wales. Man is an intermediate host for this tapeworm, along with sheep, cattle and pigs. Inadvertent ingestion of eggs passed in the faeces of an infected dog is followed by the development of so-called hydatid cysts in major organs such as the lungs and liver, necessitating surgical removal. Dogs become infected through eating raw meat containing hydatid cysts. Cooking will kill hydatid cysts so general advice is to avoid feeding raw meat and offal in areas of high risk.

There are specific requirements for treatment with praziquantel within 24 to 48 hours of return into the UK under the PETS. This is to prevent the inadvertent introduction of *Echinococcus multilocularis,* a tapeworm carried by foxes on mainland Europe which is transmissible to humans, causing serious or even fatal liver disease.

Most puppies will carry a burden of roundworm.

Roundworms (nematodes)

These are the spaghetti-like worms which you may have seen passed in faeces or brought up in vomit. Most of the de-worming treatments in use today cause the adult roundworms to disintegrate, thankfully, so that treating puppies in particular is not as unpleasant as it used to be!

Most puppies will have a worm burden, mainly of a particular roundworm species (*Toxocara canis*) which reactivates within the dam's tissues during pregnancy and passes to the fetuses developing in the womb. It is therefore important to treat the dam both during and after pregnancy, as well as the puppies.

Professional advice is to continue worming every one-to-three months, depending on perceived risk. There are roundworm eggs in the environment and, unless you examine your dog's faeces under a microscope on a very regular basis for the presence of roundworm eggs, you will be unaware of your dog having picked up roundworms, unless he should have such a heavy burden that he passes the adults.

It takes a few weeks from the time that a dog swallows a mature Toxocara canis roundworm egg to himself passing viable eggs. These

Heartworm

Heartworm infection has been diagnosed in dogs all over the world. There are two prerequisites: presence of mosquitoes, and a warm humid climate.

When a female mosquito bites an infected animal, it acquires *Dirofilaria immitis* in its circulating form, as microfilariae. A warm environmental temperature is needed for these microfilariae to develop into the infective third-stage larvae (L3) within the mosquitoes, the so-called intermediate host.

L3 larvae are then transmitted by the mosquito when it next bites a dog.

Heartworm infection is not currently a problem in the UK, except for those dogs contracting it while abroad without suitable preventative treatment. Global warming and its effect on the UK's climate, however, could change that.

It is a potentially life-threatening condition, with dogs of all breeds and ages being susceptible without preventative treatment. The larvae can grow to fourteen inches within the right side of the heart, causing primarily signs of heart failure and ultimately liver and kidney damage. It can be treated but prevention is a better plan.

For dogs travelling to heartworm-endemic areas of the EU such as the Mediterranean coast, preventative treatment should be started before leaving the UK and maintained during the visit. Again, this is best arranged with your vet.

Spot-on treatment is very effective in preventing infestation from fleas.

eggs are not immediately infective to other animals, requiring a period of maturation in the environment which is primarily temperature dependent and therefore shorter in the summer (as little as two weeks) than in the winter (several months). It is worth noting that the eggs can survive in the environment for two years and more.

There are de-worming products available which are active all the time, which will provide continuous protection when administered as often as directed. Otherwise, treating every month with an oral de-worming drug (tablet, liquid or paste) will, in effect, cut in before a dog could theoretically become a source of roundworm eggs to the general population.

It is the risk to human health which is so important: T. canis roundworms

will migrate within our tissues and cause all manner of problems, not least of which (but fortunately rarely) is blindness. The incidence in humans has fallen dramatically in recent years.

If a dog has roundworms, the eggs will also find their way onto his coat where they can be picked up during stroking and cuddling. Sensible hygiene is therefore important. You should always carefully pick up your dog's faeces and dispose of them appropriately, thereby preventing the maturation of any eggs present in the fresh faeces.

Fleas

There are several species of flea, which are not host-specific: not only can a dog be carrying cat and human fleas as well as dog fleas, but also the same flea treatment will kill and/or control them all. It is also accepted that environmental control is a vital part of a flea control programme. This is because the adult flea is only on the animal for as long as it takes to have a blood meal and to breed; the remainder of the life cycle occurs in the house, car, caravan, shed...

There is a vast array of flea control products available, with various routes of administration: collar, powder, spray, 'spot-on', oral. Since flea control needs to be applied to all pets in the house, and that is independent of whether they leave the house since fleas can be introduced into the house by other pets and their human owners, it is best to discuss your specific flea control needs with your veterinary surgeon.

Mites

There are five types of mite which can affect dogs:

(i) The mite **Demodex canis** is a normal inhabitant of canine hair follicles, passed from the bitch to her pups as they suckle. The development of actual skin disease or demodicosis depends on the individual. It is seen frequently around the time of puberty and after a bitch's first season, associated with hormonal changes. There may, however, be an inherited weakness in an individual's immune system enabling multiplication of the mite. The localised form consists of areas of fur loss without itchiness, generally around the face and on the forelimbs, and 90 per cent will recover without treatment.

The other 10 per cent develop the juvenile-onset generalised form, of which half will recover spontaneously. The other half may be depressed, go off their food, and show signs of itchiness due to secondary bacterial skin infections. Treatment is often prolonged over several months and consists of regular bathing with a specific miticidal shampoo, often clipping away fur to improve access to the skin, together with a suitable antibiotic by mouth. There is also now a licensed 'spot-on' preparation available. Progress is monitored by examination of deep skin scrapings for the presence of the mite; the initial diagnosis is based upon abnormally high numbers of the mite, often with live individuals being seen. There is a third group of individuals developing demodicosis for the first time in middle-age (more than about

Skin disease may develop after a bitch has had her first season.

four years of age), and as the generalised form. This is often reflecting underlying immunosuppression by an internal disease process such as neoplasia, or treatment with corticosteroids, for example, so it is important to identify any predisposing cause and correct it where possible, as well as specifically treating as above.

(ii) **Sarcoptes scabei** characteristically causes an intense pruritus or itchiness in the affected dog, causing the dog to incessantly scratch and bite at himself, leading to marked fur loss and skin trauma. Initially starting on the elbows, ear flaps and hocks,

without treatment the skin on the rest of the body can become involved, with thickening and pigmentation of the skin. Secondary bacterial infections are common.

Unlike Demodex, this mite lives at the skin surface, and it can be hard to find in skin scrapings. It is therefore not unusual to treat a patient for sarcoptic mange (scabies) based on the appearance of the problem even with negative skin scraping findings, and especially if there is a history of contact with foxes which are a frequent source of the scabies mite. It will spread between dogs and can therefore also be found in situations where large numbers of dogs from different backgrounds are mixing together. It should be noted that it will cause itchiness in humans, although the mite cannot complete its life cycle on us, so treating all affected dogs should be sufficient. Fortunately, there is now a highly effective 'spot-on'

Regular grooming will help you to keep a check on your Stafford's coat and skin condition.

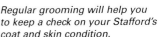

treatment for Sarcoptes scabei.

(iii) **Cheyletiella yasguri** is the fur mite most commonly found on dogs. It is often called 'walking dandruff' because it can be possible to see collections of the small white mite moving about over the skin surface. There is excessive scale and dandruff formation, and mild itchiness. It is important as a zoonosis, being transmissible to humans where it causes a pruritic rash.

Diagnosis is by microscopic examination of skin scrapings, coat combings and sticky tape impressions from the skin and fur. Treatment is with an appropriate insecticide, as advised by your veterinary surgeon.

Ears should be checked on a regular basis to ensure that they are free from infection.

(iv) A highly transmissible otitis externa (outer ear infection) results from the presence in the outer ear canal of the ear mite **Otodectes cynotis**, characterised by exuberant production of dark ear wax. The patient will frequently shake his head and rub at the ear(s) affected. The mites can also spread on to the skin adjacent to the opening of the external ear canal, and may transfer elsewhere, such as to the paws.

When using an otoscope to examine the outer ear canal, the heat from the light source will often cause any ear mites present to start moving around. I often offer owners the chance to have a look because it really is quite an extraordinary sight! It is also possible to identify the mite from ear wax smeared onto a slide and examined under a microscope.

Cats are a common source of ear mites. It is not unusual to find ear mites during the routine examination of puppies and kittens.

Ticks are more likely to affect dogs living in rural areas.

Treatment options include specific ear drops acting against both the mite and any secondary infections present in the auditory canal, and certain 'spot-on' formulations. It is vital to treat all dogs and cats in the household to prevent re-cycling of the mite between individuals.

(v) The free-living mite **(Neo-) Trombicula autumnalis** or harvest mite can cause an intense local irritation on the skin. Its larvae are picked up from undergrowth, so they are characteristically found as a bright orange patch on the web of skin between the digits of the paws. It feeds on skin cells before dropping off to complete its life cycle in the environment.

Its name is a little misleading because it is not restricted to the autumn nor to harvest-time; I find it

on the ear flaps of cats from late June onwards, depending on the prevailing weather. It will also bite humans.

Treatment depends on identifying and avoiding hotspots for picking up harvest mite, if possible. Checking the skin, especially the paws, after exercise and mechanically removing any mites found will reduce the chances of irritation, which can be treated symptomatically. Insecticides can also be applied – be guided by your veterinary surgeon.

Ticks

There were said to be classic pockets of ticks in the UK, such as the New Forest and Thetford Forest, but they are actually found nationwide. The life cycle is curious: each life stage takes a year to develop and move on to the next. Long grass is a major habitat. The vibration of animals moving

The responsible owner should be aware of the more common ailments that affect dogs.

through the grass will stimulate the larva, nymph or adult to climb up a blade of grass and wave its legs in the air as it 'quests' for a host to latch on to for its next blood meal. Humans are as likely to be hosts, so ramblers and orienteers are advised to cover their legs when going through rough long grass, tucking the ends of their trousers into their socks.

As well as their physical presence causing irritation, it is the potential for disease transmission which is of concern. A tick will transmit any infection previously contracted while feeding on an animal: for example Borrelia burgdorferi, the causal agent of Lyme disease (see page 95).

There are highly effective insecticides available and you can remove a tick manually. It is simple – provided your dog will stay still. The important rule is to twist gently so that the tick is persuaded to let go with its mouthparts. Grasp the body of the tick as near to your dog's skin as possible, either between thumb and fingers or with a specific tick-removing instrument, and then rotate in one direction until the tick comes away. I keep a plastic tick hook in my wallet at all times.

A-Z OF COMMON AILMENTS

Anal sacs (Impacted)

The anal sacs lie on either side of the back passage or anus at approximately four- and eight-o'-clock, if compared with the face of a clock. They fill with a particularly pungent fluid which is emptied onto the faeces as they move past the sacs to exit from the anus. Theories abound as to why these sacs should become impacted periodically and

Give your dog a thorough check over if he has been exercising in areas where there is long, seeded grass.

seemingly more so in some dogs than others. The irritation of impacted anal sacs is often seen as 'scooting', when the back side is dragged along the ground. Some dogs will gnaw at their back feet or over the rump.

Increasing the fibre content of the diet helps some dogs; in others, there is underlying skin disease. It may be a one-off occurrence for no apparent reason. Sometimes, an infection can become established, requiring antibiotic therapy which may need to be coupled with flushing out the infected sac under sedation or general anaesthesia. More rarely, a dog will present with an apparently acute-onset anal sac abscess which is incredibly painful.

Diarrhoea
Cause and treatment much as Gastritis (see page 112).

Ear infections
The dog has a long external ear canal, initially vertical then horizontal, leading to the eardrum which protects the middle ear. If your Stafford is shaking his head, then his ears will need to be inspected with an auroscope by a veterinary surgeon in order to identify any cause, and to ensure the eardrum is intact. A sample may be taken from the canal to be examined under the microscope and cultured to identify causal agents before prescribing appropriate ear drops containing antibiotic, anti-fungal agent and/or steroid. Predisposing causes of otitis externa or infection in the external ear canal include:
• presence of a foreign body such as a grass awn;
• ear mites which are intensely irritating to the dog and stimulate the production of brown wax, predisposing to infection;
• previous infections causing the canal's lining to thicken, narrowing the canal and reducing ventilation;
• swimming – some Staffords will swim, but water trapped in the external ear canal can lead to infection, especially if the water is not clean!

Foreign bodies

There are two type of foreign bodies that may affect your Stafford:

Internal: Items swallowed in haste without checking whether they will be digested can cause problems if they lodge in the stomach or obstruct the intestines, necessitating surgical removal. Acute vomiting is the main indication. Common objects I have seen removed include stones from the garden, peach stones, babies' dummies, golf balls, and once a lady's bra ...

It is possible to diagnose a dog with an intestinal obstruction across a waiting room from a particularly 'tucked-up' stance and pained facial expression. These patients bounce back from surgery dramatically. A previously docile and compliant obstructed patient will return for a post-operative check-up and literally bounce into the consulting room.

External: Grass awns are adept at finding their way into orifices such as a nostril, down an ear, and into the soft skin between two digits (toes), whence they start a one-way journey due to the direction of their whiskers. In particular, I remember a grass awn which migrated from a hindpaw, causing abscesses along the way but not yielding itself up until it erupted through the skin in the groin!

Gastritis

This is usually a simple stomach upset, most commonly in response to dietary indiscretion. Scavenging constitutes a change in the diet as much as an abrupt switch in the food being fed by the owner. There are also some specific infections causing more severe gastritis/enteritis which will require treatment from a veterinary surgeon (see also Canine Parvovirus under Vaccination earlier).

Generally, a few days of small, frequent meals of a bland diet such as cooked chicken or fish or an appropriate prescription diet should allow the stomach to settle. It is vital to ensure the patient is drinking and retaining sufficient to cover losses resulting from the stomach upset in addition to the normal losses to be expected when healthy. Oral rehydration fluid may not be very appetising for the patient, in which case cooled boiled water should be offered. Fluids should initially be offered in small but frequent amounts to avoid over-drinking which can result in further vomiting and thereby dehydration and electrolyte imbalances.

When returning the patient back on to routine food, it is vital to wean over gradually or else another bout of gastritis may occur.

Joint problems

It is not unusual for older Staffords to be stiff after exercise, particularly in cold weather. This is not really surprising, given that they are such busy dogs when young. This is such a game breed that a nine or ten year old Stafford will not readily forego

Lumps and bumps

Regularly handling and stroking your dog will enable the early detection of lumps and bumps. These may be due to infection (abscess), bruising, multiplication of particular cells from within the body, or even an external parasite (tick). If you are worried about any lump you find, have it checked by a veterinary surgeon.

an extra walk, or take kindly to turning for home earlier than usual. Your veterinary surgeon will be able to advise you on ways for helping your dog cope with stiffness, not least of which will be to ensure that he is not overweight. Arthritic joints do not need to be burdened with extra bodyweight!

Obesity

Being overweight does predispose to many other problems such as diabetes mellitus, heart disease and joint problems. It is so easily prevented by simply acting as your Stafford's conscience. Ignore pleading eyes and feed according to your dog's waistline.   The body condition is what matters qualitatively, alongside monitoring that individual's bodyweight as a quantitative measure. The Stafford should, in my opinion as a health professional, have at least a suggestion of a waist and it should be possible to feel the ribs beneath only a slight layer of fat.

Neutering does not automatically mean that your Stafford will be overweight. Having an ovario-hysterectomy does slow down the body's rate of working, castration to a lesser extent, but it therefore means that your dog needs less food, a lower energy intake. I recommend cutting back a little on the amount of

A well-balanced diet and regular exercise should keep your Stafford at the correct weight.

food fed a few weeks before neutering to accustom your Stafford to less food. If she looks a little underweight on the morning of the operation, it will help the veterinary surgeon as well as giving her a little leeway weight-wise afterwards.

It is always harder to lose weight after neutering than before, because of this slowing in the body's inherent metabolic rate.

Teeth problems

Eating food starts with the canine teeth gripping and killing prey in the wild, incisor teeth biting off pieces of food and the molar teeth chewing it. To be able to eat is vital for life, yet the actual health of the teeth is often over-looked: unhealthy teeth can predispose to disease, and not just by reducing the ability to eat. The presence of infection within the mouth can lead to bacteria entering the bloodstream and then filtering out at major organs, with the potential for serious consequences. That is not to forget that simply having dental pain can affect a dog's well-being, as anyone who has had toothache will confirm.

Veterinary dentistry has made huge leaps in recent years, but. good dental health lies in the hands of the owner. In an ideal world, we should brush our dogs' teeth as regularly as our own. The Stafford puppy who finds having his teeth brushed is a huge game and excuse to roll over and over on the ground requires loads of patience, twice a day.

There are alternative strategies ranging from dental chew-sticks to specially formulated foods, but the main thing is to be aware of your dog's mouth. At least train your puppy to permit full examination of his teeth, which will not only ensure you are checking in his mouth regularly but also make your vet's job easier when there is a real need for your dog to 'Open wide!'

We are fortunate that the Stafford is a hardy breed with few inherited disorders.

INHERITED DISORDERS

Any individual, dog or human, may have an inherited disorder by virtue of genes acquired from the parents. This is significant not only for the health of that individual but also because of the potential for transmitting the disorder on to that individual's offspring and to subsequent generations, depending on the mode of inheritance.

There are control schemes in place for some inherited disorders. In the

US, for example, the Canine Eye Registration Foundation (CERF) was set up by dog-breeders concerned about heritable eye disease, and provides a data-base of dogs who have been examined by diplomates of the American College of Veterinary Ophthalmologists.

As well as screening programmes, it is now possible to directly identify the genes responsible for certain inherited disorders. This means that, by running DNA tests before

With careful screening, only the healthiest stock goes forward for breeding.

breeding, individuals carrying unwanted genes can be identified and breeding programmes designed accordingly. All that is required is a blood sample and/or a cheek swab, depending on the condition being assessed, procedures which are generally well tolerated.

To date, only a few conditions have been confirmed in the Stafford as being hereditary. In alphabetical order, these include the following:

L-2-Hydroxyglutaric Aciduria (L2-HGA)

This is a so-called metabolic disorder with serious, distressing consequences. There is a wide range of signs which may be shown by an affected individual. These include behavioural changes and dementia (for example, staring blankly at the wall, or becoming so disorientated and confused by his surroundings as to become

Hereditary and juvenile cataracts

This is not a congenital condition; there is juvenile-onset of progressive development of cataracts in the lenses of both eyes, commonly quoted as starting at five to eight months of age, but which may actually be detected at as early an age as three or four weeks. Affected individuals will be total blind by the age of between one and three years. HC is inherited as an autosomal recessive, and carriers can now be identified with a DNA test (from The Animal Health Trust, Newmarket in the UK) to ensure they are only bred with clear individuals. There is also classic certification under Schedule A of the BVA/KC/ISDS* Eye Scheme.

marooned under a table or in a corner of the room), anxiety attacks, reduced ability to exercise, wobbly gait (ataxia) and muscular stiffness, tremors or full seizures (so it can be mistaken for epilepsy).

It is inherited as an autosomal recessive, meaning that both parents must be carriers (or affected) for an individual to manifest the disorder. A DNA test (from The Animal Health Trust, Newmarket in UK) is now available to identify carriers to ensure they are only bred to clear individuals which will avoid the production of affected offspring. Totally excluding carriers from breeding programmes could adversely affect the breed by restricting the gene pool available and therefore limiting natural genetic diversity.

Patellar luxation

This is the condition which I point out to my children when I spot a dog walking along the road, giving a little hop for a few steps every now and again. The kneecap or patella is slipping out of position, locking the knee or stifle so that it will not bend and causing the characteristic hopping steps until the patella slips back into its position over the stifle joint. Fortunately, it is not very common in the Stafford. Surgical correction is possible in severely affected dogs, but many simply carry on intermittently hopping, the long-term effect inevitably being arthritis of the stifle.

Persistent Hyperplastic Primary Vitreous (PHPV)

Affected individuals retain the developmental blood supply to the lens to a varying degree in one or both eyes. Since these vessel remnants lie within the line of vision, sight will be affected to a variable degree. Fortunately, it can be so mild as to cause no sight impairment. PHPV is not in itself progressive, although blindness can result from haemorrhage within the eye and cataract formation.

The mode of inheritance involved in PHPV is unclear. Since it is a congenital fault, present at birth, puppies can be examined and affected individuals identified from six weeks of age under Schedule A of the BVA/KC/ISDS* Eye Scheme.

Posterior Polar Subcapsular Cataract (PPSC)

This is a form of cataract occurring in other breeds which has been an incidental finding in only a few Staffords during screening examination for HC and PHPV (see above).

Hips and elbows can be scored using X-rays.

Overlong soft palate

This is considered hereditary and does occur in other brachycephalic breeds such as the Bulldog and Pekinese. It is seen only rarely in the Stafford, suggested by some to be a reflection of his more pronounced vertical 'stop', although a cluster occurred a few years ago in related Staffords.

Elbow and Hip dysplasia

These are inherited orthopaedic disorders which show a spectrum of changes, and can be crippling. There is instability of the malformed joints, such that arthritis develops in an attempt to achieve better stability but may simply contribute to or worsen the level of pain. The degree of change seen radiographically is not necessarily a good guide to the effect on the individual: a dog with a very high hip score may not be as lame as a dog with a lower one, hence the need for a standardised scoring/grading system.

Any breed can be screened for Elbow and Hip dysplasia under the BVA/KC** schemes in the UK, not currently a requirement for the Stafford by the Kennel Club's Accredited Breeder Scheme. As of 1st November 2007, a relatively small number of Staffords (44) had had their hips scored, giving a mean total score of 13 with a range of 6 – 47, the worst possible total score being 106 and the best zero.

In the US, assessment of the Stafford's elbows and hips is more routine, with approximately 80 per cent grading normal for either/both.

*British Veterinary Association/Kennel Club/International Sheepdog Society
** British Veterinary Association/Kennel Club

Complementary therapies can be of great value when used in conjunction with conventional veterinary care.

COMPLEMENTARY THERAPIES

Just as for human health, I do believe there is a place for alternative therapies but alongside and complementing orthodox treatment under the supervision of a veterinary surgeon. That is why 'complementary therapies' is a better name.

Because animals do not have a choice, there are measures in place to safeguard their wellbeing and welfare. All manipulative treatment must be under the direction of a veterinary surgeon who has examined the patient and diagnosed the condition which she or he feels needs that form of treatment. This covers physiotherapy, chiropractic, osteopathy and swimming therapy. For example, dogs with arthritis who cannot exercise as freely as they were accustomed will enjoy the sensation of controlled non-weight-bearing exercise in water, and benefit with improved muscling and overall fitness.

All other complementary therapies, such as acupuncture, homeopathy and aromatherapy, can only be carried out by veterinary surgeons who have been trained in that particular field.

Acupuncture is mainly used on dogs for pain relief, often to good effect. The needles look more alarming to the owner, but they are very fine and are well tolerated by most canine patients. Speaking personally, superficial needling is not unpleasant and does help with pain relief.

Homeopathy has had a mixed press in recent years. It is based on the concept of treating like with like. Additionally, a homeopathic remedy is said to become more powerful the more it is diluted.

If you have any concerns regarding your Stafford's health, do not delay in seeking veterinary advice.

CONCLUSION

As the owner of a Stafford, you are responsible for his care and health. Not only must you make decisions on his behalf, you are also responsible for establishing a life-style for him which will ensure he leads a long and happy life.

Diet plays as important a part in this as exercise, for example. Nutritional manipulation has a long history. Formulation of animal feedstuffs is aimed at optimising production from, for

A Stafford that is well cared for should live a long life and suffer few health problems.

neutered or are less active than others, or simply like their food. Do remember, though, that ultimately you are in control of your Stafford's diet, unless he is able to profit from scavenging!

On the other hand, prescription diets are of necessity fed under the supervision of a veterinary surgeon because each is formulated to meet the very specific needs of particular health conditions. Should a prescription diet be fed to a healthy dog, or to a dog with a different illness, there could be adverse effects.

example, dairy cattle. For the domestic dog, it is only in recent years that the need has been recognised for changing the diet to suit the dog as he grows, matures and then enters his twilight years. So-called life-stage diets try to match the nutritional needs of the dog as he progresses through life.

An adult dog food will suit the Stafford living a standard family life. There are also foods for those Staffords tactfully termed as obese-prone such as those who have been

It is important to remember that your Stafford has no choice. As his owner, you are responsible for any decision made so it must be as informed a decision as possible. Always speak to your veterinary surgeon if you have any worries about your Stafford. He is not just a dog, because he will have become a member of the family from the moment you brought him home.

Useful Addresses

BREED & KENNEL CLUBS
Please contact your Kennel Club to obtain contact
information about breed clubs in your area.

UK
The Kennel Club (UK)
1 Clarges Street London, W1J 8AB
Telephone: 0870 606 6750
Fax: 0207 518 1058
Web: www.thekennelclub.org.uk

USA
American Kennel Club (AKC)
5580 Centerview Drive, Raleigh, NC 27606.
Telephone: 919 233 9767
Fax: 919 233 3627
Email: info@akc.org
Web: www.akc.org

United Kennel Club (UKC)
100 E Kilgore Rd, Kalamazoo,
MI 49002-5584, USA.
Tel: 269 343 9020
Fax: 269 343 7037
Web:www.ukcdogs.com/

AUSTRALIA
Australian National Kennel Council (ANKC)
The Australian National Kennel Council is the
administrative body for pure breed canine affairs in
Australia. It does not, however, deal directly with dog
exhibitors, breeders or judges. For information
pertaining to breeders, clubs or shows, please contact
the relevant State or Territory Body.

Dogs Australian Capital Territory
PO Box 815, Dickson ACT 2602
Tel: (02) 6241 4404
Fax: (02) 6241 1129
Email: administrator@dogsact.org.au
Web: www.dogsact.org.au

Dogs New South Wales
PO Box 632, St Marys, NSW 1790
Tel: (02) 9834 3022 or 1300 728 022 (NSW Only)
Fax: (02) 9834 3872
Email: info@dogsnsw.org.au
Web: www.dogsnsw.org.au

Dogs Northern Territory
PO Box 37521, Winnellie NT 0821
Tel: (08) 8984 3570
Fax: (08) 8984 3409
Email: admin@dogsnt.com.au
Web: www.dogsnt.com.au

Dogs Queensland
PO Box 495, Fortitude Valley Qld 4006
Tel: (07) 3252 2661
Fax: (07) 3252 3864

Email: info@dogsqueensland.org.au
Web: www.dogsqueensland.org.au

Dogs South Australia
PO Box 844, Prospect East SA 5082
Tel: (08) 8349 4797
Fax: (08) 8262 5751
Email: info@dogssa.com.au
Web: www.dogssa.com.au

Tasmanian Canine Association Inc
The Rothman Building
PO Box 116, Glenorchy Tas 7010
Tel: (03) 6272 9443
Fax: (03) 6273 0844
Email: tca@iprimus.com.au
Web: www.tasdogs.com

Dogs Victoria
Locked Bag K9, Cranbourne VIC 3977
Tel: (03)9788 2500
Fax: (03) 9788 2599
Email: office@dogsvictoria.org.au
Web: www.dogsvictoria.org.au

Dogs Western Australia
PO Box 1404, Canning Vale WA 6970
Tel: (08) 9455 1188
Fax: (08) 9455 1190
Email: k9@dogswest.com
Web: www.dogswest.com

INTERNATIONAL
Fédération Cynologique Internationalé (FCI)
Place Albert 1er, 13, B-6530 Thuin, Belgium.
Tel: +32 71 59.12.38
Fax: +32 71 59.22.29
Web: www.fci.be/

TRAINING AND BEHAVIOUR

UK
Association of Pet Dog Trainers
Telephone: 01285 810811
Web: http://www.apdt.co.uk

Association of Pet Behaviour Counsellors
Telephone: 01386 751151
Web: http://www.apbc.org.uk/

USA
Association of Pet Dog Trainers
Tel: 1 800 738 3647
Web: www.apdt.com/

American College of Veterinary Behaviorists
Web: http://dacvb.org/

American Veterinary Society of Animal Behavior
Web: www.avsabonline.org/

AUSTRALIA
APDT Australia Inc
Web: www.apdt.com.au

Canine Behaviour
For details of regional behvaiourists, contact the
relevant State or Territory Controlling Body.

ACTIVITIES

UK
Agility Club
http://www.agilityclub.co.uk/

British Flyball Association
Telephone: 01628 829623
Web: http://www.flyball.org.uk/

USA
North American Dog Agility Council
Web: www.nadac.com/

North American Flyball Association, Inc.
Tel/Fax: 800 318 6312
Web: www.flyball.org/

AUSTRALIA
Agility Dog Association of Australia
Tel: 0423 138 914
Web: www.adaa.com.au/

NADAC Australia (North American Dog Agility
Council - Australian Division)
Web: www.nadacaustralia.com/

Australian Flyball Association
Tel: 0407 337 939
Web: www.flyball.org.au/

INTERNATIONAL
World Canine Freestyle Organisation
Tel: (718) 332-8336
Web: www.worldcaninefreestyle.org

HEALTH

UK
Alternative Veterinary Medicine Centre
Tel: 01367 710324
Web: www.alternativevet.org/

British Small Animal Veterinary Association
Tel: 01452 726700
Web: http://www.bsava.com/

Royal College of Veterinary Surgeons
Tel: 0207 222 2001
Web: www.rcvs.org.uk

USA
American Holistic Veterinary Medical Association
Tel: 410 569 0795
Web: www.ahvma.org/

American Veterinary Medical Association
Tel: 800 248 2862
Web: www.avma.org

American College of Veterinary Surgeons
Tel: 301 916 0200

Toll Free: 877 217 2287
Web: www.acvs.org/

AUSTRALIA
Australian Holistic Vets
Web: www.ahv.com.au/

Australian Small Animal Veterinary Association
Tel: 02 9431 5090
Web: www.asava.com.au

Australian Veterinary Association
Tel: 02 9431 5000
Web: www.ava.com.au

Australian College Veterinary Scientists
Tel: 07 3423 2016
Web: http://acvsc.org.au

ASSISTANCE DOGS

UK
Canine Partners
Tel: 08456 580480
Web: www.caninepartners.co.uk

Dogs for the Disabled
Tel: 01295 252600
Web: www.dogsforthedisabled.org

Guide Dogs for the Blind Association
Tel: 01189 835555
Web: www.guidedogs.org.uk/

Hearing Dogs for Deaf People
Tel: 01844 348100
Web: www.hearingdogs.org.uk

Pets as Therapy
Tel: 01845 345445
Web: http://www.petsastherapy.org/

Support Dogs
Tel: 01142 617800
Web: www.support-dogs.org.uk

USA
Therapy Dogs International
Tel: 973 252 9800
Web: www.tdi-dog.o

Therapy Dogs Inc.
Tel: 307 432 0272.
Web: www.therapydogs.com

Delta Society - Pet Partners
Web: www.deltasociety.org

Comfort Caring Canines
Web: www.comfortcaringcanines.org/

AUSTRALIA
AWARE Dogs Australia, Inc
Tel: 07 4093 8152
Web: www.awaredogs.org.au/

Delta Society —Therapy Dogs
Web: www.deltasociety.com.au

Index

Contributors

THE AUTHOR: CLARE LEE (CONSTONES)

Clare grew up with Staffords belonging to her father, Nap Cairns. In the 1960s she and her husband, Tony, joined with her father in the Constones prefix. This is now the oldest, active prefix in the breed and has produced several Champions and show winners, with dogs of Constones breeding producing many more Champions of their own.

Clare has been judging at Championship level for nearly 40 years, including at Crufts 1985 – the fiftieth anniversary year of the breed's recognition. She has judged throughout Europe, as well as in Australia, Russia, Canada, the US and South Africa.

For a number of years Clare was Secretary of the Northern Counties SBT Club, of which she has been made a Life Vice President. She has written/edited two books on the Breed and is the present breed correspondent for the Dog World weekly journal.

Additional material for Chapter Five contributed by Shirley Gray (Bullmaple).

ALISON LOGAN MA VetMB MRCVS

Alison qualified as a veterinary surgeon in 1989 . She has been in practice in her home town ever since, living with her husband, two children and Labrador Retriever Pippin. She contributes on a regular basis to Veterinary Times, Veterinary Nurse Times, Dogs Today, Cat World and Pet Patter, the PetPlan newsletter. In 1995 and 2002, Alison won the Univet Literary Award, later known as the Vetoquinol Literary Award. See Chapter Six: Health Care for Staffords.

Further Reading

The Staffordshire Bull Terrier
(BEST OF BREED)

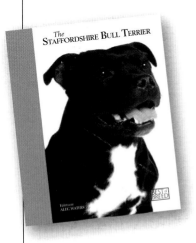

Written by leading experts, including the late Alec Waters, *The Staffordshire Bull Terrier* offers readers an unrivalled depth of knowledge about their chosen breed. The book gives detailed information on character and behaviour, puppy care, training and socialisation, with a special chapter on Staffordshire health written by a leading vet. Illustrated by a stunning collection of more than 120 specially commissioned colour photographs, matched by the high-specification production, and distinctively finished with real cloth binding, this is one breed book no Stafford lover should be without.

Puppy Raising Made Easy

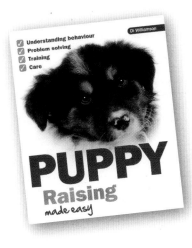

Puppy Raising Made Easy is a fully comprehensive guide to raising and training a puppy, covering everything from choosing the right breed to dealing with problem behaviour.

Divided into seven easy-to-follow chapters, the book examines puppy behaviour and deals with practical concerns, such as feeding, exercise and travelling, as well as explaining how to manage typical puppy issues, such as play-biting and house training.

The author describes how to maximise training success and provides detailed instructions for teaching your puppy basic obedience commands, including Sit, Down, Stay and Retrieve, as well as practical advice about encouraging simple good manners in your dog, such as meeting people in a well-behaved manner and walking nicely on the lead. Lastly, there is a chapter about what to do when things go wrong, providing sensible guidelines for dealing with problem behaviour.

Puppy Raising Made Easy contains everything you need to raise a well-mannered, obedient companion. If you only buy one puppy training book, make it this one.

Veterinary Advice For Dog Owners

Veterinary Advice for Dog Owners is a comprehensive guide to canine health and illness.

- Part one covers all aspects of caring for your dog to keep him fit and healthy, including preventative health care.
- Part two comprises a detailed breakdown of the dog's physiology and how disease and disorder affects it.
- Part three looks at the rise in popularity of complementary health therapies and how they can work alongside traditional veterinary treatments to maximise the dog's recovery and well-being.

Written by well-respected vet and author Dick Lane, *Veterinary Advice for Dog Owners* is a canine health guide no dog lover can afford to be without.